THE CORPORATION
OF LEICESTER
1689–1836

THE CORPORATION
OF LEICESTER
1689–1836

R. W. GREAVES

LEICESTER UNIVERSITY PRESS
1970

First published in 1939 as part of the
Oxford Historical Series
(*Editors:* G. N. Clark, C. R. Cruttwell, F. M. Powicke)
Second edition published in 1970 by
Leicester University Press

Distributed in North America by
Humanities Press Inc., New York

Printed in Great Britain by Stephen Austin & Sons Ltd.

ISBN 0 7185 1071 2

This reprint has been authorized by
The Clarendon Press Oxford

PREFACE

THE following study is based on a dissertation submitted for the degree of D.Phil. In the course of its preparation I have incurred many debts of gratitude. Most of the researches on which it is based were made while I held a Harmsworth Senior Scholarship at Merton College. Miss L. Stuart Sutherland has given me the most generous assistance at all stages of my work, and to her I am most especially grateful. I am indebted also to Professor G. N. Clark for the considerable help he has given me; and to Mr. David Ogg and Dr. E. G. Dowdell for useful criticisms of my original version. Miss Christine Ellis, Mr. R. L. Ager, Dr. Ivy Pinchbeck, Mr. J. S. Elliott, Mr. S. E. Gunn, and Mr. F. J. G. Cook read my typescript at various stages of its preparation, and I appreciate their interest, suggestions, and criticisms.

Mr. H. A. Pritchard, formerly Town Clerk at Leicester, was very kind in securing me access to the archives in his custody, and Mr. Walker and his colleagues in the Town Clerk's office did a good deal to make my visits congenial as well as useful. Miss A. P. Deeley and Miss E. Swift, successively Archivists at the Leicester Museum, and Mr. Cox and his colleagues at the Leicester Central Library all bore with my unusual demands most patiently and helpfully. The incumbents of Leicester Cathedral, S. Nicholas', S. Mary de Castro, and All Saints', Leicester, namely the Very Rev. F. B. Macnutt, the Rev. Canon Berridge, the Rev. J. R. Collins, and the Rev. F. T. Ingle, and as well Mr. E. Morris, clerk to S. Margaret's Select Vestry, all very readily and kindly gave me access to their parochial records.

I hope that those of my friends who have helped me, but who are not mentioned here by name, will understand that they also have been of real assistance, for which I am grateful.

This book is dedicated to the memory of my Mother.

R. W. G.

BEDFORD COLLEGE,
REGENT'S PARK, N.W. I.

PREFACE TO SECOND EDITION

In this edition the bibliography contained in the original edition has been omitted. The bibliographical references are sufficiently indicated in the footnotes. Since 1939, the following works have appeared to which attention should be drawn.

The Victoria County History of Leicestershire, vol. III (1955), and vol. IV (1958). In particular, vol. IV, pp. 110–21 elucidates the history of the charters of the town, and especially that of 1688.

R. W. Greaves, 'Roman Catholic Relief in the Leicester Election of 1826', *Transactions of the Royal Historical Society*, 4th series, xxii (1940), 199–223.

R. W. Greaves, 'The Old Leicester Corporation and the Town Almshouses' in *Transactions of the Leicestershire Archaeological Society*, xxi (1940), 149–73.

A. Temple Patterson, *Radical Leicester* (Leicester, 1954).

G. B. A. M. Finlayson, 'The Municipal Corporations: Report. 1833–5', *Bulletin of the Institute of Historical Research*, xxxvi (1963), 36–52.

G. B. A. M. Finlayson, 'The Politics of Municipal Reform 1835', *English Historical Review*, lxxxi (1966), 673–92.

The appendix of lists and select documents given in the first edition seems no longer necessary, now that publication is continuing of the *Records of the Borough of Leicester* edited by G. A. Chinnery; volumes V and VI have already appeared, and volume VII is in preparation.

Further information about the parliamentary representatives for the Borough may now be found in L. B. Namier and John Brooke: *History of Parliament: The House of Commons 1754—1790* (1964).

I am greatly indebted to Professor J. Simmons and Dr Aubrey Newman for their generous help in the preparation of this new edition.

R.W.G.

UNIVERSITY OF KANSAS
LAWRENCE, KANSAS
NOVEMBER 1969

CONTENTS

ABBREVIATIONS

Bodl. = Bodleian Library.

CA. = MS. Chamberlains' Accounts.

Gardiner = W. Gardiner, *Music and Friends.*

HB. = MS. Hall Books.

HCJ. = *House of Commons Journals.*

HLJ. = *House of Lords Journals.*

HMC. = Historical Manuscripts Commission.

HP. = MS. Hall Papers.

Hartopp, *Register* = *Register of the Freemen of the Borough of Leicester.*

Hartopp, *Mayors* = *Roll of the Mayors of Leicester.*

MCR. = Report of the Commissioners on Municipal Corporations, 1835.

Nichols = *History and Antiquities of the County of Leicestershire.*

Records = *Records of the Borough of Leicester,* vols. i–iii ed. by Mary Bateson, vol. iv by H. Stocks.

SR. = MS. Sessions Rolls.

Searson = *Twenty-five Years of Liberalism in Leicester.*

Throsby, *History* = *History of Leicester.*

Throsby, *Memoirs* = *Memoirs.*

Thompson = *History of Leicester in the Eighteenth Century.*

ELG. = S. and B. Webb, *English Local Government.*

i.	*Parish and County.*
ii and iii.	*Manor and Borough.*
iv.	*Statutory Ad Hoc Authorities.*
v.	*The King's Highway.*
vi.	*English Prisons.*
vii.	*Old Poor Law.*

INTRODUCTORY

THE English municipal corporations of the eighteenth century, responsible for only a small part of the field of local government, remained somewhat out of the main stream of events until the radical agitations of the early railway age made them a matter of common interest. The self-electing aldermen and councilmen of 1835 were still following a routine hardly different from that which their forebears had observed at the time William of Orange had landed in England a century and a half before. The growth of industry, the loss of one empire and the winning of another, even the counter-revolutionary panic that followed from the French revolution and revolutionary wars, had in general less effect on the local municipal oligarchies than upon the townspeople at large. Indeed, in Leicester the constitutional structure of local government was less affected by these profound changes than it was in most towns. For there was there an almost unique absence of statutory local authorities for public improvement.

Local autonomy and local isolation, the general absence of popular control, meant that the corporations of the English towns tended to become, in varying degrees, exclusive political clubs, concerned chiefly with the upholding of their civic dignity, the disposal of their patronage, the increase of their civic properties and revenues, the maintenance of their independence, if it were not already lost, against the local aristocracy, and the promotion of the correct political opinions, 'whig', or 'tory', or merely 'corporation party', as the case might be, at parliamentary elections. The increase of population, commerce, and industry reduced these ancient and unchanging institutions to an overripe obsolescence. In the eighteen-twenties the storm of reforming agitation broke upon them. Demands were made that the untidiness of great local variety should be reduced to order, and that municipal corporations should be amenable to popular control and serve more efficiently the purposes of local government in the towns, which were for the most part dirty and unsafe. A start in bringing order out of municipal confusion had already been made

in the previous century by the great Lord Mansfield, who had
by his decisions aimed to build up a comprehensive body of
law appertaining to municipal corporations. His decisions
formed a basis for such nineteenth-century writings as the
legal collection of Willcock and, to a less extent, the
historical collection of Merewether and Stephens, which,
though academic in form, had the ulterior purpose of
embellishing legal material with comments designed 'to
influence public opinion in favour of municipal reform'.[1]
Thus lawyers from the outset had a prominent part in the
overthrow of the old corporate system.[2]

The corporation of Leicester, the special object of this
study, is of great interest for the light it throws on rather
different aspects of the old system and its reform, especially
on the local roots of the reform agitation and on the social
and political animosities behind the fight for the supremacy
of the ratepayer in the nineteenth-century town. Throughout the eighteenth century the corporation of Leicester
appears as a typical municipal oligarchy; but in the twenties
of the next century, as the most notorious of all corporations, it became a symbol for the old corporate system,
talked of by all political persons. Our study therefore falls
naturally into two parts. First, we have to survey in
general the corporation's chief activities, its difficulties and
policies, and to observe how, as the eighteenth century
progressed, the municipality grew more and more out of
contact with the town community as a whole. In so doing
we shall obtain a cross-section of an interesting phase of
eighteenth-century social life, so remarkably different from
the life of Victorian and post-Victorian England. Especially
we shall notice the internal tensions that accentuated the
general inefficiency of out-of-date administrative arrangements. Then, in our second part, we have to observe the
changing political life of the town, and especially its

---

[1] H. A. Merewether and A. J. Stephens, *History of the Boroughs and Municipal
Corporations of the United Kingdom* (1835); J. W. Willcock, *Municipal Law*
(1827); the phrase quoted is from C. Gross, *Bibliography of Municipal History*
(1897), xxv, used by Gross of the first of the works cited in this note.

[2] Another well-known expression of the reforming spirit amongst lawyers is
J. Chitty, *A Practical Treatise on the Law relative to Apprentices and Journeymen,
and to exercising Trades* (1812), especially pp. 1–7.

becoming gradually dominated, to the exclusion of all else, by a political and sectarian conflict to which the corporation was a party—a conflict so bitter that local feuds penetrated even the walls of Westminster, and so irreconcilable that it could only be resolved by municipal revolution. The Leicester corporation had a greater part than any other single municipal body in the last conflicts of the old toryism with the reformers.

I

TOWN AND CORPORATION

EDUCATED inhabitants of Leicester for long prided themselves on its antiquity as a place inhabited since the earliest period of English history. Its ancient municipal corporation gloried in having existed 'from time immemorial'.[1] Parson Carte, who in the first half of the eighteenth century investigated the antiquities of the town where he had become 'rector of the chief church',[2] wrote for his friend the antiquary Browne Willis an account in which he dilated on the Roman and Saxon remains, the Norman castle, abbey, and churches, the benefactions of sixteenth-century patrons, and the growing importance of the town reflected in the charters of Elisabeth.[3] His account has been of great value to subsequent writers and is embodied in the monumental compilation of Nichols.[4]

Carte was not, however, so much the priest and antiquary that he did not observe the source of a good deal of the material well-being of the town in his own day. For he noted the growing importance of the local stocking-making industry, and as well the multiplying population, then about 6,450 inhabitants, enough for a moderate-sized village of the present age, but by 1835 increased by six times.[5] In Carte's time, and until the Municipal Reform Act of 1835, this increasing population was distributed between the ancient parishes of the town, six in number, and the outlying districts, which lay for the most part within these parochial areas, but outside the borough jurisdiction, namely the various liberties.[6] Throughout the whole of our period the borough of Leicester, it is important to notice, was thus 'by no means co-extensive with the town'.[7]

---

[1] MCR. 1890, 'Leicester is a borough by prescription.'

[2] Bodl. MS. Carte 244, fo. 77; the 'chief church' being S. Martin's, now Leicester Cathedral.

[3] Bodl. MS. Willis LXXXV.

[4] Cf. C. J. Billson, *Leicester Memoirs* (1924), 131–2.

[5] MCR. 1890: citing census of 1831, as giving population at 38,904.

[6] MS. Willis LXXXV, fo. 20; see below for the great importance of the liberties in the constitutional problems of the town, pp. 35–9, 41 ff.

[7] MCR. 1889.

There were certain features of the life of this small country town that distressed Samuel Carte. Its isolation, separated by bad roads from the intellectual life of the universities and the metropolis, made his scholarly activities at times difficult to maintain, especially as the local book-sellers were far from academic.[1] The small circle of local life could be very dull, yet was subject to the most violent disturbance by the heat of faction, increased by the malicious omniscience of country-town gossip. Above all, amongst the respectable shopkeepers, though not amongst the inn-keepers, and amongst the industrial workers who went to make up the community of the town there was a regrettably strong element of religious nonconformity. From the last decades of the sixteenth century, when the puritan Henry, third earl of Huntingdon, founded a civic lecturership, to be filled by puritan preachers, until the Restoration, it appears that both town and corporation remained strong-holds of puritanism.[2] So far as the town as a whole was concerned, protestant nonconformity, a residuary legatee of the once dominant sectaries, remained still very strong. It won a final victory in the events that close our study in 1836. It was otherwise with the corporation. By 1689 that had become a clearly tory body.

The official description of the corporation of Leicester was as ' the Mayor Bailiffs and Burgesses of the Borough of Leicester ', a style conformable to the charter of 1599.[3] The corporation itself consisted, along with the executive officers, of the two companies of common councilmen and of aldermen, respectively of forty-eight and twenty-four members. The twenty-four were chosen out of the forty-eight ; the forty-eight out of the main body of the freemen, who, as the town grew in size, formed a diminishing pro-portion of the whole population.[4] The corporate body was also self-electing. Out of the aldermen were chosen the mayor, and out of the common council the two chamber-lains. In addition there were other officers : the two

---

[1] MS. Willis XLVIII, fo. 363, S. Carte to Browne Willis, 12 Mar. 1715/6.
[2] *Records*, III. xxiii. 118, 226. [3] *Records*, III. 359–64.
[4] Cf. MCR. 1897 ; the number of freemen resident was 1,569 in 1832, and within seven miles 2,070 ; the total number being between four and five thousand. The population of the town was then over 38,900.

bailiffs, appointed alternately by the earls of Huntingdon and the corporation; a town clerk and a town solicitor; a recorder and a steward. There was also the usual retinue of mace-bearers and other minor servants.[1]

The history of the Leicester corporation during the two hundred years before the revolution of 1688 is one of increasing exclusiveness, as its institutions received greater definition at the hands of the legislature and the Crown. 'There was', it has been well said, 'simply no other channel open than the line of becoming more select and exclusive.'[2] Thus, to condemn the unreformed corporations for being unrepresentative is to apply to them democratic criteria which were the product of later circumstances.[3]

The two conciliar bodies of forty-eight and twenty-four had different origins. The older of the two, the twenty-four, was the original common hall, and its origin is a matter of controversy. Bateson held that it grew out of a coalescence of the gild's morningspeche and the ancient burghal portmanmote.[4] The most recent writer on the subject, Dr. Tait, finds in Leicester the gild playing the chief part in the development of municipal freedom, though he would not go so far as the Leicester historian James Thompson in generalizing from the Leicester material about the influence of gilds merchant in general.[5] The Leicester common council consisted at first of twenty-four *jurati*, known later as aldermen, and was from the outset, as Bateson insists,[6] a close and not a popularly elected body. In Tait's view it was a peculiarity of the Leicester common council that 'it originated in the merchant gild, which had grasped administrative control of the town'.[7] Even Gross, who led the attack on Thompson's identification of the gild with the burgess community, commented on the 'abnormal predominance' of the gild at Leicester.[8]

[1] MCR. 120, 1895.
[2] M. Weinbaum, *The Incorporation of Boroughs* (Manchester, 1937), 26; cf. 122–4.
[3] Cf. K. B. Smellie, *A Hundred Years of English Government* (1937), 11–12.
[4] *Records*, II. xliii–xlvi.
[5] J. Tait, *The Mediaeval English Borough* (Manchester, 1936), 222–34, especially pp. 232–4.
[6] *Records*, II. xlvi.   [7] Tait, op. cit. 274.
[8] C. Gross, *Bibliography of Municipal History* (1897), xxviii.

Bateson also noted that in Leicester tasks fell to the gild which did not normally elsewhere fall to these merchant bodies.[1] Yet even in Leicester the gild had nothing to do with the administration of civil and criminal law.[2] There was thus in the municipal arrangements at Leicester a constitutional duality with an element of gild predominance. This was in our period still, as we shall see, of importance for the corporation.[3]

To the original body of twenty-four there was added by legislation of Henry VII, applying to Leicester and Northampton, in consequence of disturbances at the elections of mayors,[4] a second body, of forty-eight common councillors, to speak for the commonalty. This new body was, like the senior company, a close body from the outset, 'chosen, not by the burgesses at large, but by the then existing governing body, the Mayor and Four and Twenty',[5] in whom this power remained till 1835. Except for the short period of Charles II's charter, Leicester, unlike Northampton,[6] retained this bicameral constitution given to it in the law of 1489. The two charters of Elisabeth, of 1589 and 1599, both continued the forty-eight and twenty-four,[7] but with one slight but significant alteration. While the act of 1489 had spoken of the forty-eight as 'acting for the whole body of the town', the charter of 1589 incorporated the mayor and his companies as 'burgesses', so 'reducing the rest of the population to the status of mere inhabitants'.[8] The new company of common councilmen remained in a definitely subordinate place in the local corporation. Its importance was to some slight extent increased by James I's charter of 1609, which provided that the twenty-four senior members of the forty-eight should join with the aldermen to form the body of commissioners for letting and setting the town lands.[9]

---

[1] *Records*, I. xxxi.   [2] C. Gross, *The Gild Merchant* (1890), i. 65, 87.
[3] It had its bearing on the important case of *Blankley* v. *Winstanley*; see p. 38.
[4] Tait, op. cit. 323; *Records*, II. 285, 319; MCR. 1892: Private Acts 4 Hen. VII, §§ 22–3.
[5] *Records*, II. xlvi–xlix, lv.
[6] MCR. 1966: governing charter of 36 George III (1796).
[7] *Records*, III. 247–52, 359–64.   [8] Tait, op. cit. 323; *Records*, III. 248.
[9] *Records*, IV. xxxiii. 80–1.

The exclusiveness of the Leicester corporation which was its chief characteristic in the eighteenth century was thus no new feature, nor was it created by the Stuart manipulation of municipal bodies. What becomes more pronounced in the Restoration period in Leicester is the partisanship of the corporation. Apparently during the interregnum, as we have seen, the leanings of the Leicester corporation had been to the puritan side, no doubt not uninfluenced by pressure from the military.[1] Consequently there followed, under the Corporation Act of 1661, a purging out of puritan members, who could not receive the Holy Communion after Anglican rites.[2] 'The two companies were so drastically remodelled that out of seventy-two members in November 1660, forty were struck off the rolls, and of these fifteen were aldermen.'[3] Thus, although the religious tests of the later Caroline system do not appear to have been always strictly enforced before 1689,[4] a definitely Anglican party character was given to the Leicester corporation.

None the less, it would not be true to say that there was thereby created a cleavage between a corporation of tory churchmen and a town community of largely whig and nonconformist opinions. There was a considerable body of tory churchmanship in the town at large, and the puritans and dissenters, powerful though they were to become, were probably at the most only a large minority. The strongest evidence of this is to be found in the charter of Charles II, which in 1684 remodelled the corporation. Besides replacing the old forty-eight and twenty-four by new companies of twenty-four and thirty-six, this new charter changed the character of the parliamentary franchise. For by direction of Charles II the parliamentary franchise was taken out of the hands of the two companies, who had exercised it during the interregnum,[5] and vested in the commonalty of scot and lot payers at large.[6] To make this arrangement the government must have felt par-

---

[1] Cf. *Records* IV. liii. 379–81, 383.
[2] Cf. *EHR*. xlv (1930), 237 ff., especially 251 ff.
[3] *Records*, IV. lv. 479–80, 606–7.   [4] Ibid. lv. 498, 505–7.
[5] Cf. ibid. 419–20.   [6] Ibid. 576.

ticularly certain of the political and ecclesiastical character of the majority of the Leicester electorate,[1] since the general tendency of Charles II's changes was to restrict, and not to expand, the franchise.[2] The divergence of politics between the corporation and the town community, and therefore the unrepresentativeness of the municipal body, was not then, we may conclude, as great in 1689 as it later became. One of the tasks of this essay will be to explain some of the chief causes of that growing divergence.

The charter of 1684 had only a short life, and James II's charter of 1688 was abortive. When James II in a panic of concession annulled all municipal charters granted since 1679[3] the Leicester municipality in consequence of his proclamation reverted to the form it had been given by Queen Elisabeth.[4] There were not in Leicester the disputes between rival corporations, claiming under old and new charters, that took place in some other towns.[5]

It is important to notice that throughout all these changes the corporation retained its close character. Nor was the position of the aldermen weakened by these vicissitudes. As was designed by the governing charter of 1599, the company of twenty-four aldermen enjoyed, until the end of the unreformed corporation's life, predominant authority and were 'more specifically the governing body'.[6] Thus there were not in Leicester the unedifying contentions between the two companies that from time to time vexed Warwick[7] or Norwich, at which latter place the two companies had actually opposing political allegiances.[8] Such factions as there were had to find leaders among the aldermen. Generally personal or political, these dissensions commonly concentrated in some constitutional or legal issue. Thus in 1766 political dissension[9] led to the

---

[1] Ibid. lv.

[2] *EHR.* xlv. 242, citing *Cal. of State Papers Dom. 1660–1*, p. 582, and cf. *EHR.* xlv. 245.

[3] G. N. Clark, *The Later Stuarts 1660–1714* (1934), 130.

[4] *Records*, IV. 589.

[5] For the interesting case of Bewdley, *ELG.* ii. 270, note 3 ; for other instances see the paper, 'The Convention Parliament', by J. H. Plumb, *Cambridge Historical Journal*, v (1937), 238, note 20.

[6] *HLJ.* lxvii. 389; *Records*, III. 361.

[7] MCR. 2058, 2071.   [8] *ELG.* iii. 545–6, 549–50.   [9] See below, pp. 102–3.

dismissal of common councilman John Pocklington and alderman James Sismey, respectively for insolvency and non-residence, and their enforced reinstatement by means of a writ of mandamus from King's Bench.[1] Again, in 1774 dispute arose about the right of dismissing town servants at pleasure, whether it lay in the mayor alone or jointly in the mayor and aldermen acting together.[2] This was finally settled by the court of aldermen in 1799 in favour of the mayor alone.[3]

Apart from these occasional crises, the main features of interest in the month-by-month routine of the common halls are two developments, both of which we may associate with an increasing amount of business coming before the meetings during the eighteenth century. The first was a stricter organization of the meetings. In 1689 the standing orders were added to by a rule that reflects not too well on the social standing and manners of some of the members, namely that members must not attend the hall not wearing bands,[4] and in 1708 rules were drawn up to secure orderly observance of the conventions of debate.[5] In 1765[6] and in 1797[7] the standing orders were thoroughly revised, and in 1819 it was ordered that each meeting should begin by the reading of the minutes.[8] This latter rule was no doubt of great practical importance, for now the minutes had become imposing and detailed records, including often reports of great value to the student.

The second group of orders arose from the difficulty of recruiting the common halls. There were, it is true, sometimes signs of competition to join the common council,[9]

---

[1] HB. 10 Sept. 1766. These charges were obviously pretexts, as both Sismey and Pocklington had been appointed to serve on a committee on 22 Nov. 1765: HB. 25 May 1767 for the mandamus and reinstatement; cf. Merewether and Stephens, *History of the Boroughs and Municipal Corporations of the United Kingdom* (1835), i. 250. This was a case of some legal importance: 4 Burr. 2087: Willcock, *Municipal Law* (1827), § 672, p. 259.

[2] Press 24 (4), case of *Pinder* v. *Billing*.   [3] HB. 22 July 1799.

[4] HP. xx, fo. 134; at a common hall, 1 May 1689; stated to be 'according to a former order'; cf. *Records*, IV. lvi–lvii.

[5] HP. xxi, common hall, 6 Jan. 1707/8.

[6] HB. 22 Nov. 1765.   [7] HB. 26 Sept. 1797.   [8] HB. 26 Aug. 1819.

[9] Cf. HP. xxii, court of aldermen (9 June 1696); HB. 10 Sept. 1714; 29 July 1720—this period seems to have been the most prosperous part of our period for the corporation.

no doubt in consequence of the policy of spending corporation money with corporation members, 'they selling as cheap as other tradesmen '.[1] But the signs of reluctance are more frequent. At the beginning of our period the purgings and remodellings of corporate bodies in the seventeenth century had increased the unpopularity of municipal service by rendering its benefits uncertain. Consequently, in 1690 it was necessary for an order to be made at Leicester for the fining of the recalcitrant,[2] after the fashion well established in the English borough corporations.[3] Later, when corporation business was heavy, in 1760-2, Robert Peach resisted for two years.[4] Finally, in 1762 a general order was made fixing the fine for refusal at thirty pounds.[5] These refusals are understandable in view of the loss that might come to a tradesman's business as a result of his spending much time at corporation meetings, civic services, and public banquets. Further, elections to common hall often meant the first step to more exalted office, which made greater demands on pocket and time.

Every corporation had of necessity at its head a group of executive officials, varying in size and personnel from borough to borough. In Leicester this group was comparatively large, consisting of the mayor and chamberlains and the town clerk and solicitor.

The mayor as 'persona' of the corporation occupied a place of great dignity and of considerable legal importance,[6] although in Leicester his influence was comparatively limited. He was not, like some other mayors, either keeper of the jail or coroner, and his influence in the

---

[1] e.g. HB. 20 Oct. 1697. [2] HB. 29 Sept. 1690.
[3] *ELG.* ii. 392; iii. 469, 698, 699 n. 2.
[4] HB. Feb. 1760–Oct. 1762; Peach afterwards became mayor in 1786.
[5] HB. 4 Mar. 1761, 2 Aug. 1762.
[6] Cf. J. W. Willcock, *Municipal Law* (1827), § 94, p. 53; §§ 129–32, pp. 68–9: lays down that the mayor's presence is necessary for the lawful transaction of business in a corporate assembly. The statute 11 Geo. I, c. 4, provides a procedure for the election of a mayor, in default of election on the proper charter day, by mandamus obtained from King's Bench; cited by Willcock, § 534, p. 211, in discussing this contingency. The Leicester corporation offers illustration of this in the failure of David Harris in 1810 to be sworn on the proper day on account of his wife's illness at Brighton, HB. 8 Oct. 1810.

market was limited by special officers there.[1] In fact there was, at Leicester as generally elsewhere, between 1689 and 1835 a certain 'decline in the importance of the mayoralty',[2] to be ascribed usually to the growing authority of the magistrates in sessions, and to the determined corporate control of municipal property.[3] Various attempts were made in Leicester to control the exercise of the mayoral discretion, by the passing of general orders of the hall,[4] and even, on one occasion, of an order for the withholding of a third of the salary on account of an irregularity in the mayor's administration of the apprenticeship law.[5]

By virtue of his office the mayor was involved in expenditure not merely of time but also of money. A salary was therefore necessary. At the beginning of our period the mayor received £40 a year. This sum was made up of three equal parts, one paid by the corporation, the second paid to him as master of Trinity hospital out of hospital revenues, and the third out of the rent of the Gosling close as a payment for binding apprentices. An attempt was made to end the second of these in 1778, when the duchy of Lancaster held that the mayor had no right to a salary as master of the hospital.[6]

None the less, the mayor's salary steadily mounted. The municipal commissioners reported in 1835 that the mayor received £242 4s. 10d. a year.[7] The new town council of 1836, by taking into account the mayor's newspaper allowance and his retaining in his hands, on provision of security, without payment of interest, three to five thousand pounds, the balance of Sir Thomas White's charity, arrived at an estimate of from £360 to £460.[8] This was undoubtedly a comparatively generous salary,

---

[1] See below, p. 63.   [2] *ELG.* ii. 315.   [3] See below, pp. 78–9.
[4] e.g. HB. 6 Mar. 1703/4, 14 July 1722.   [5] See below, pp. 51–2.
[6] The Chamberlains' Books of Payments of 1789 and 1822 both record the hospital salary as an item to be paid to the mayor, but it is not mentioned in MCR. It looks rather as if the salary continued to be paid, illegally. BM. Add. MSS. 38446, fo. 77 ; cf. *Records*, IV. 211.
[7] MCR. 1900.
[8] MS. Council Minutes, 13 Jan. 1836. It is perhaps worth noting that similar conditions prevailed in administrative departments of the government : e.g. the pay office as found by the elder Pitt.

more than was paid by most corporations, but not so much as was paid in some.[1]

What the zealous reformers of 1835 overlooked was the great expense attached to the mayoralty. There were mayors who after their term of office could not pay twenty shillings in the pound. John Goodall, mayor in 1680 and again in 1690, petitioned for dismissal from the body in 1699, as having 'served all the offices in this corporation, both to the loss of his time and expense of money'.[2] Edmund Johnson, mayor in 1711, could only pay ten shillings in the pound.[3] John Cartwright, mayor in 1771, was not able to pay debts due to Gabriel Newton, contracted several years before, and was compelled by adverse circumstances to resign from the corporation.[4] John Pocklington, mayor in 1778, in 1789 only paid eleven and threepence in the pound on a debt of £20 due to Trinity hospital, and died a poor man, a pensioner of the corporation.[5] To the conscientious the mayoralty involved the fulfilment of expensive and burdensome obligations. It was 'an honorary office of considerable personal labour'.[6]

At least equally overburdened, and quite unpaid, were the two chamberlains. Their office in Leicester was not, as in London,[7] a place of profit to be competed for, but a place of labour to be avoided if possible. The two chamberlains of Leicester were appointed, one for the mayor and the other for the commonalty, according to an arrangement that dated back to the fifteenth century.[8] Their duties were set forth in their oath,[9] and were comprehensive enough. First, the chamberlains were to attend the mayor on all lawful occasions and to obey his lawful

---

[1] Cf. *ELG.* ii. 315–16.   [2] HP. xx, fo. 116; Hartopp, *Mayors*, 113–14.
[3] HB. 27 Dec. 1717, 9 Apr. 1718; CA. 1716–17, 1717–18; Thompson, 36–7.
[4] PRO. C12/443/20; Hartopp, *Mayors*, 164; *Trans. Leics. Arch. Soc.* xix (1936–7), pt. ii, 362.
[5] HB. 29 Sept. 1789, 6 Jan. 1797, 27 Jan. 1804; Hartopp, *Mayors*, 167.
[6] *ELG.* ii. 316.
[7] *ELG* iii. 684.
[8] *Records*, ii, lii; cf. also MCR. 1892 for an ascription of this arrangement to the sixteenth century: and a criticism of this in *Records*, iii. xxviii and note.
[9] MS. Oath Book.

commands; second, they were to 'maintain and improve the Merchant Gild and the lands and tenements belonging to the said Borough';[1] third, they were to help in the organizing of the markets; and fourth, they were to make all collections and disbursements of money for the corporation and the gild and to draw up accounts to be submitted to the annual audit.

The office of chamberlain, like that of mayor, could on occasion be filled only by compulsion.[2] Thus, in 1711 it was only after four attempts, with steadily mounting fines, that a chamberlain was found,[3] and in 1800 recourse was even had to the threat of a writ of mandamus.[4] An arduous office, rewarded by no perquisites, it had its own special difficulties, particularly on the financial side.

It cannot be said that the accounts of the corporation were kept scientifically, and to judge from the extant accounts, the annual audit was often perfunctory. Further, since the corporation often found difficulty in balancing its budget,[5] and in the hands of a chamberlain the public and private purses could easily be confused, there were occasions of inconvenience, if not of dishonesty, and very likely of financial loss to the chamberlain. In view of these circumstances, it is specially noteworthy that a committee of 1811 could report on 'the integrity and fairness with which the accounts now are and have been conducted'.[6]

The audit was the means of getting the accounts made up, and the expenses of it were the only allowance made to the chamberlains.[7] Time had often to be extended to allow the chamberlains to finish their book-keeping,[8] but

---

[1] *Records*, II. xliii. 193, 321.

[2] HB. 21 Sept. 1777 at £10 10s.: order for subsequent fining at £30, though this order was not enforced. HB. 21 Sept. 1778, when John Dalby was fined at 10 guineas. HB. 21 Sept. 1793, fine raised to £20. HB. 31 July 1805, fine made £30.

[3] HB. 21 Sept. 1711. [4] HB. 29 Sept. 1800. [5] See below, p. 56.

[6] HB. 26 Feb. 1811. The value of this committee's opinion is perhaps not great; see below, pp. 15, 18.

[7] MCR. 1896 states that apparently no salary was paid to the chamberlains; cf. *Records*, III. xxviii. HB. 28 Feb. 1728/9 speaks of the chamberlains' salary as increasing from £7 to £12.

[8] HB. 11 Feb. 1708/9, 13 Jan. 1719/20, 31 July 1805.

it was even more difficult on occasion to get the balance paid over due to the corporation from the outgoing chamberlain, especially if his private affairs were going badly. Thus in 1725[1] and in 1741[2] chamberlains were compelled by threat of legal action to pay the balance due in instalments. In 1778 instalments were spread over more than a year, and on about a third of the whole sum due only fifteen shillings in the pound was paid.[3]

Further difficulty arose when chamberlains of moderate means, not receiving the balance of the previous year's accounts, had to draw on their private resources.[4] Consequently, in 1782, an order was made for £100 always to be paid to incoming chamberlains,[5] a policy further extended in 1804[6] and in 1805.[7] It is not surprising therefore that from time to time the common hall should seek to regulate by general order how money should be spent,[8] and should have appointed between 1799 and 1832 a series of finance committees,[9] even if these bodies had little effect and the last two never met at all.[10] For a more uneconomical mode of business could hardly have been devised. The finances of an ancient, dignified, and propertied corporation were conducted on lines not substantially different from those of some fugitive college literary club.

The vast quantity of work resting on the shoulders of honorary and unprofessional officers who, though they were commonly not unconscientious, were often muddled and inevitably incompetent, had one disastrous consequence. The unprofessional dignitaries fell too much under the sway of the corporation's professional officers, especially of the town clerk. The influence of the town clerk was, as we shall see, a by no means negligible factor

---

[1] HB. 25 Mar. 1725.   [2] HB. 2 Feb. 1740/1.   [3] HB. 28 Aug. 1778.
[4] HB. 3 Feb. 1791, a chamberlain compensated for advances made by him.
[5] HB. 5 Dec. 1782.
[6] HB. 25 Sept. 1804, a second £100 payable in December.
[7] HB. 31 July 1805, a third £100 payable on 30 Nov.
[8] e.g. HB. 23 July 1716, no allowance for payments except when receipted bills were produced; HB. 17 Oct. 1750, any proposed expenditure to be authorized by the common hall.
[9] HB. 7 Mar. 1799, to discuss purchase of land tax; HB. 26 Feb. 1811, an important body to deal with the increased income from the south field.
[10] *Leicester Chronicle*, 12 Oct. 1833.

in the final disgrace of the old corporation of Leicester. Nor was this undue influence checked by any degree of popular control.

By 1689 the town clerk had already superseded in importance the steward of the borough court, who had been intended under the charter of Elisabeth to serve as the chief day-to-day legal adviser of the corporation.[1] During the eighteenth century the town clerkship undoubtedly grew in importance, and in value to its holder. For whereas John Boley, appointed in 1702, had to be buried at the corporation's expense,[2] his office by the end of the century was a useful piece of patronage in the hands of party politicians.[3] It was by then valuable enough to be held by members of the dignified Heyrick family.[4] Its value was still further increased when over the turn of the century it absorbed the parallel office of town solicitor.[5]

The most conclusive evidence of the increase of the town clerkship is financial. In 1711, apart from legal fees, which in a litigious age were generally considerable,[6] the only fixed salary of the town clerk was £16 13s. 4d. William Heyrick in 1811 secured so substantial an increase that thenceforward the town clerk enjoyed a fixed salary of £200.[7] Yet this £200 was a mere fraction of the total income enjoyed by the town clerk as a result of his town clerkship. Besides legal fees for corporation business

[1] *Records*, III. 362; *ELG.* ii. 325-6.

[2] HB. 18 Sept. 1702, 10 Oct. 1712, salary increased to £5 yearly; 5 Apr. 1715, Boley granted £5 for better maintenance during his own and his wife's illness; 25 June 1715, the hall grants £2 for funeral expenses.

[3] Leic. Mus. MSS. Berridge, 109'30/34'8, also 109'30/34'9; correspondence about the suspected inclination of John Heyrick to the 'Bakewellite' side in 1765-6.

[4] Heyricks held legal offices in the corporation from 1737 till the end of the century; see the lists in Nichols, i. 454.

[5] This process apparently complete by Caleb Lowdham's retirement; Lowdham appears as still doing corporation business in 1808, in connexion with alderman Newton's charity; see W. E. Beasley, *History of a Leicester Firm of Attorneys* (Leicester, 1930), 12-14. The two offices were certainly combined by William Heyrick, appointed town clerk HB. 10 Feb. 1791.

[6] e.g. CA. 1766-7, legal expenses to Halford and Heyrick, solicitor and clerk respectively, amounted to £215 19s. 9d., besides other costs of a legal kind amounting to £59 13s. 2d. and £30 in bills to the town clerk. CA. 1754-5, solicitor Halford's bill of charges £183 16s. 4d.

[7] HB. 26 Feb., 8 Apr. 1811.

there were payments for legal business transacted for the parishes of the town, and the income of various minor offices commonly held by the town clerk. Consequently the town clerk enjoyed a very large income, so that the last town clerk of the old corporation, Thomas Burbidge, claimed under the compensation clause of the Municipal Reform Act[1] for loss of his office on the basis of his income for the years 1831–4 no less a sum than £10,870 6s. 1d. in salary and legal charges. He had also held on behalf of Sir Thomas White's and alderman Newton's charities £10,000, of which he had stopped £4,000 for bills that the corporation had never seen.[2]

Thomas Burbidge in fact illustrates a cardinal weakness of the old system. Overworked unprofessional officers, dependent in numerous problems for professional advice on their servant the town clerk, and unsupported by any close contact with alert opinion in the town community at large, were in a defenceless position, open to be hoodwinked by the unscrupulous, as they certainly were by Burbidge. 'In Borough towns,' quote the Webbs from a contemporary account, 'particularly those called close, . . . a want of education, intelligence &c. . . . too frequently places the Corporate Leader in the hands of a crafty Town Clerk.'[3]

The career of Thomas Burbidge shows also that the influence of the town clerk was to no appreciable extent limited by the increase that took place in the professional staff of the corporation during the eighteenth century, with the appointment of a land steward[4] and additions to the market staff.[5] Nor was it appreciably affected by an equally interesting development, in the direction of a system of committees, with the double object of economizing the time of the common hall and of limiting the discretion of individual officers. At Leicester the corporation never developed so impressive a system of committees as, for instance, functioned at Norwich[6] or in such towns as had

---

[1] 5 & 6 Will. IV, c. 76, § 66.

[2] MS. Council Minutes 1836–9, *passim*; *Examination of Thomas Burbidge*, pp. 41–2.

[3] *ELG*. iii. 697.   [4] See below, pp. 78–9.   [5] See below, p. 63.

[6] *ELG*. iii. 543–4; P. Milligan, *Register of the Freemen of Norwich 1548–1713* (Norwich, 1934), xii–xx.

active committees of trade.[1] At Leicester all was haphazard, *ad hoc*.

The greatest of the Leicester committees was the south field committee. This, with a nucleus dating from 1795, by various stages reached its final form by 1805.[2] Originally, as its name indicates, it was started to deal with the south field inclosures ;[3] but in the course of time it showed a tendency to engross business that appears hardly germane to its original purpose.[4] The activities of this committee aroused the jealousy of the body of commissioners for letting the town lands, which, unlike the committee, could claim the authority of letters patent of James I for its supervision of the municipal estates.[5] Its protest reflects also no doubt a fear that a small clique might monopolize an advantageous control of borough property at the expense of other members. Consequently, in 1812, the two bodies were made identical, the commissioners to be the south field committee, five being a quorum.[6] As appears from the minutes, this change did not go without protest. At any rate, it did not apparently make much difference.

There were also attempts to form a permanent committee of account, for the more systematic ordering of corporation finance,[7] but apparently without success. In the last decade of the old corporation's life attempts to form finance committees were usually the outcome of political crisis.[8] They never succeeded in affecting any even temporary improvement in the financial arrangements of the corporation. There is unfortunately no evidence to show how far their working was hindered by such persons as Burbidge, who profited out of chaos and extravagance.

---

[1] e.g. Oxford, 'for the purpose of superintending & preserving the exclusive privilege of the freemen to carry on trade in Oxford', MCR. 100. See *ELG.* ii. 283.

[2] For the earlier committees which were of a temporary character, the evidence is in HB. 1795–7; for the permanent committee, HB. 19 Dec. 1805, appointed on lines suggested by a committee of 1803, HB. 9 Sept. 1803.

[3] See below, pp 80–6.

[4] e.g. HB. 9 Mar. 1810, erection of guard- and watch-houses in the town; HB. 14 Mar. 1825, letting town lands at Bushby.

[5] See above, p. 7.   [6] HB. 29 July 1812.   [7] HB. 26 Feb. 1811.

[8] HB. 27 Aug. 1828, after the election of 1826, which was critical for the corporation; HB. 29 Mar. 1832, no doubt in view of the approaching election.

Some other committees were probably more useful, though not all have left many traces on the minutes. Such were committees for pavements, for markets, for alderman Newton's charity, as well as the body of ex-mayors for the governance of the free grammar school.[1]

We may see in these attempts to organize the corporation's business the members of the common hall labouring to adapt an inherited system of unpaid and compulsory service, in a close and irresponsible body, to the great changes that took place between 1688 and 1835. The corporation did not lack a sense of obligation to the community at large. Difficulties arose partly because the strictly legal obligations of the body were not, as they are after the modern manner, clearly defined, but still more because the members of the body, with the institutions at their command, had but little chance of success, especially in view of the fierce political factions that divided the town.

[1] HB. 24 Jan. 1713/14; it was decided by a majority of 8 to 3 at a meeting of the mayor and aldermen that the mayor and ex-mayors appointed the head-master. Previous usage on this point was not consistent, Nichols, i. 512, cf. *Charity Commissioners' Report*, 32, part v (1838), 6; the mayor and ex-mayors assumed also the right of appointing the undermasters, HB. 28 June 1714; previous appointments had been made by the hall, HB. 11 Oct. 1689, 16 Mar. 1701/2, 6 May 1713. This illustrates the growing concentration of power in the hands of the few senior members of the body.

II

THE BOROUGH MAGISTRACY

SO far our study of the common halls has led us merely to notice a piecemeal adaptation of traditional routine to increasing business. In coming to consider the borough magistracy we are introduced to more crucial problems which go much farther to explain the ferocity of party conflict in the Leicester of the early nineteenth century, and the catastrophic collapse of the old corporation.

The Webbs have argued that what distinguished the genuine municipal corporation from the highly developed manorial borough was the existence in a town of a system whereby members of the corporation were automatically appointed to serve as justices of the peace for the borough. It is especially important for the student of eighteenth-century Leicester to notice also that along with the privilege granted to a number of municipal boroughs to hold courts of quarter sessions went also the power in boroughs enjoying county status of levying a county rate, or, in those not of county status, of levying a rate 'of the nature of a county rate'.[1]

Leicester was first supplied with justices of the peace in 1464 by letters patent of Edward IV, the justices to be chosen by the twenty-four.[2] In 1599, by Elisabeth's charter, this arrangement was changed. From then until the municipal reform of 1835 the town magistracy consisted of the mayor and recorder, together with the four aldermen who had last been mayor. Their jurisdiction extended 'to all cases not touching life or limb', and consequently 'to all felonies not capital'.[3] Over the borough proper the magistrates exercised an exclusive jurisdiction. On the other hand, as to the liberties there was, as we shall see, considerable dispute between town and county in the latter part of the century.

Under this arrangement the court of quarter sessions consisted exclusively of corporation men. The justices were

---

[1] *ELG.* ii. 266–7, 283, 285. [2] *Records,* ii. xliv. 281.
[3] Ibid. iii. 363; MCR. 1897.

most appropriately spoken of as the 'corporation magistrates'. For the recorder was appointed by the aldermen,[1] and the bailiff, a corporation official, in nominating the grand jury, appointed exclusively members of the forty-eight, who 'attended as corporators in their robes of office'.[2] Even the constables who made presentments to the court were nominated by the justices.[3] The only limitation on the corporation's control was the negligible one that, according to an arrangement made under James I, the earls of Huntingdon exercised the right of appointing a bailiff alternately with the corporation.[4] During the whole of the eighteenth century this right of the earl's made a difference only on one occasion, and then the incident was comparatively trifling. Leonard Piddocke, a bailiff of the earl's appointing, claimed the right of appointing the town jailer as part of his patronage, the corporation resisting this claim. The dispute was settled by a compromise; the corporation maintained the right of nomination for the bailiff to appoint, while consenting this time to nominate the bailiff's candidate.[5] Although the bailiffs had a high precedence in the corporation, their responsibilities were not great. Of the two bailiffs, the one existing only in name, the other 'ministerial', even the latter had a sinecure. After 1820 he enjoyed an annual salary of fifty guineas, while the duties of the post were performed by that Pooh-bah the town clerk, acting as under-bailiff.[6]

Thus the court of quarter sessions consisted of the most influential members of the corporation. By means of the sessions the corporation came to have a closer connexion with the provision of social services for the town. The importance of the sessions in the life of the eighteenth-century corporation can thus hardly be exaggerated. For

---

[1] *Records*, III. 362; HB., numerous references.   [2] MCR. 1897.
[3] See below, pp. 23–5.   [4] *Records*, IV. 87–9, 106.
[5] HB. 10 Dec. 1739: the common hall was divided equally between two candidates, one nominated by Piddocke; the mayor's casting vote was given against Piddocke's man; for the ensuing correspondence, HB. 11 July 1740; Throsby, *History*, 81–2: Thompson, 53–6.
[6] Press 5 (111), opinion of Sergt. Walker in *Throsby v. Bunney*, for the two bailiffs; HB. 28 Mar. 1820; MCR. 1895, 1900, for the salary. For Burbidge's position as under-bailiff, see *Examination of Thomas Burbidge*, 5–8.

it was in practice the justices that exercised the sovereignty
in the constitution of the borough. They ruled over the
parishes of the town in much the same way as their
brethren in the county. 'The borough justices of the peace',
say the Webbs, 'become more and more the dominant
influence in the municipal corporations.'[1] It was even
stated in 1833 that the justices at Leicester actually chose
who should be members of the common hall.[2]

Moreover, the court of quarter sessions completely over-
shadowed the borough court of record. This latter was the
descendant of the medieval portmanmote. It was intended
by the charter of 1599 to be held by the mayor, the recorder,
the bailiffs, the steward, or any one of them, for trying
'real, mixed and personal actions to any amount'.[3] An
expensive court, it was by the nineteenth century, in spite
of the professions of its steward,[4] in a state of decay.[5] Its
unpopularity we may infer from attempts that were made
in 1782[6] and in 1832[7] to obtain a local act for a court of
conscience at Leicester for dealing with small debts.

The court of quarter sessions had thus no rival in the
town. It had long possessed itself of the court leet's jurisdiction over nuisances.[8] Indeed, business at the sessions
grew so heavy that the plan was at times put forward of
increasing the meetings from four to six.[9] The borough
magistracy was therefore the directing body in the corporation. The magistrates, as such, figured frequently on committees that apparently had no reference to their judicial
office. Yet their position was not exactly like that of the
rural justices of the peace. For one thing, they generally
lacked the dignity and important connexions of the county
families, since they were of the tradesman class.[10] Further,
the county justices made their sessions into a kind of local
legislature. Justices in quarter sessions, it was complained,

[1] *ELG.* ii. 385–90.
[2] *Leicester Journal*, 26 Apr., 10 May 1833; see below, p. 125, n. 1.
[3] *Records*, iii. 363; MCR. 1897.   [4] HB. 11 Feb. 1818.
[5] MCR. 1895, 1897.
[6] HB. 5 Dec. 1782.
[7] *HCJ.* lxxxvii. 462, 5 July 1832.   [8] *ELG.* ii. 122–4.
[9] *Leicester Journal*, 9 May 1828, then suggested as a means of dealing with
an overcrowded jail.
[10] See Hartopp, *Mayors,* passim.

'consider themselves a sort of legislative body, and at
liberty to do whatever they please'.[1] As regards the
Leicester borough sessions it is undoubtedly unsafe to
dogmatize owing to the unfortunate state of the sessions
records ;[2] yet it seems fairly plain that the justices in their
quasi-legislative activity often preferred to work, not in
their quarter sessions, but through the common hall, in
which were passed appropriate resolutions, and which had
the power of making by-laws for sanction by the justice of
assize in circuit.[3] It may also have been that the Leicester
justices, being not uncommonly lesser men in estates and
experience, were more reluctant than the great gentry of
the county to act freely on their own initiative,[4] and in a
spirit of more timid legalism [5] stuck closely to the advice
of their legal officers, and the instructions in the various
manuals for the help of justices of the peace, which were
published during the century, and some of which were
bought for the use of the corporation.[6]

In many essentials, then, the government of Leicester
was not markedly different from that of any rural area. It
was a group of parishes immediately subject to the supervision of the local justices of the peace, except for the
difference that the justices formed the most important group
within the corporation. So it remained till the reform of
the municipal corporations, without the interposition of any
statutory *ad hoc* authority.[7] In consequence, reliance had
still to be placed for the maintenance of such social services
as there were on the medieval procedure of presentment
and indictment. In this procedure a great burden was put
on the petty constables of the town. These were appointed
in Leicester, not for the parishes, as they were in the
country-side and in many towns, but for the wards, into

[1] J. Ritson, *The Office of Constable* (1791), xxviii.
[2] They are very fragmentary.
[3] Cf. *Records*, III. 361 (charter of 1599); for the making of a by-law, see
below, p. 32.
[4] Cf. Holdsworth's comment in E. G. Dowdell, *A Hundred Years of Quarter
Sessions* (1932), lxix; and contrast *ELG*. ii. 358.
[5] A marked feature of the Leicester corporation.
[6] CA. 1707-8, purchase of Nelson's *Justice* ' for the town's use'; CA. 1755-6,
a bookseller's bill included Shaw's *Justice*.
[7] *ELG*. iii. 475-6.

which the town had been divided for police purposes in the
fifteenth century.[1]

The constables of the twelve wards, with their assistants,
or headboroughs or thirdboroughs, were appointed by the
magistrates at the quarter sessions out of three names submitted for each ward by the outgoing constable on com-
pleting his year of service.[2] The office of constable was
nowhere popular. It involved duty without dignity or
perquisite. Moreover, as Ritson argued in his classical
treatment of the subject, a post that really required intelligence and station for its adequate fulfilment was degraded
and, by the practice of paying proxies, left commonly to
the ignorant.[3]

Precepts issued to constables of wards at Leicester had
the usual common form of comprehensive exhortation.
Their recipients were burdened with a variety of duties:
to search out 'all Rogues, Vagabonds, or Idle Wandering
Beggars'; to inquire if hue and cry had been duly practised
according to law; to find out what strangers had come into
the ward, and tried 'to settle themselves therein not being
duly qualified according to law'; to discover any persons
selling ale without licence, keeping disorder in their houses,
or suffering unlawful games; and finally, to present any
other offences against the laws of the realm.[4] The poor
law, the peace, the condition of streets and roads, the conduct of public houses, the keeping of correct weights and
measures, the reporting of seditious utterances—all these
might form matter of the constable's presentment.

The constable was thus an inquisitor of the pettiest kind.
Matters too high for him, or involving persons of too high
station, were presented at the quarter sessions by the grand
jury. There is abundance of evidence that the manifold
duties of the constables were ill performed. The number
of constables' presentments testifying, with remarkable
vagaries of spelling, that all was well, 'omne bene', in
their wards is most suspiciously large. Occasionally, con-

---

[1] *Records*, II. lxvi–lxviii. 305–8.

[2] HP. xxii, by endorsement on the precepts issued to them.

[3] Ritson, op. cit. viii–xiii.

[4] HP. xxii. On this subject see also *ELG.* i. 499; Dowdell, op. cit. 19 ff.;
D. H. Marshall, *The English Poor in the Eighteenth Century* (1926), 233 ff.

stables had difficulty in exacting service from their head-borough:[1] sometimes they were themselves indicted for neglect.[2] Besides the release from this compulsory service after a year, the constable had one consolation : that he might hope to reimburse himself, at least in part, for his expenditure on holding vagrants, moving on the poor to their places of settlement, erecting stocks, and other out-lays arising from his office, by means of a rate levied on the parish and collected by the churchwardens and over-seers of the poor.[3] In immediately post-war periods, as after the peace of Ryswick, the constables' activities, and therefore their rate, were greatly increased, ' by reason of the great number of disbanded soldiers and other poor passengers '.[4]

A chief source of interest for the historical student in the local government of eighteenth-century Leicester lies in the attempts made by the justices from time to time to escape from this obsolete system. These attempts are interesting both in themselves and for the light they throw on the ultimate discredit of the Leicester corporation. All the efforts of the justices to improve the existing arrange-ments turned upon one point, their power to levy a rate. The hostility to rate-supported improvement, common in the eighteenth century, and by no means confined to Leicester,[5] accounts very largely for the unsatisfactory state of local government in the town.

[1] SR. 1757.

[2] SR. 1711, eleven constables of the wards for not presenting ' the streets within their several wards being the Queen's highway the same being very much out of repair '.

[3] Ritson, op. cit. 33 ff.; Dowdell, op. cit. 75; Marshall, op. cit. 239–41; *ELG.* i. 28. Bills of constables, for mending stocks (1699), in HP. xxiii; numerous bills in HP. xxiii–xxiv. Assessments in HP. xxii (1688, 1689). HP. xx, fo. 188, order for payment. CA. 1693–4, 1695–6, payments for constables in respect of corporation lands.

[4] HP. xxii.

[5] *ELG.* v. 22–4.

III

THE DEFEAT OF THE MAGISTRACY

TWO policies were tried by the corporation in the attempt to find a way of escape from the obsolete system inherited from its medieval and Elisabethan forebears. One was to attempt to obtain a local act establishing a body of improvement commissioners with rating powers; the other to establish on a satisfactory basis a borough rate levied by the justices themselves. Each of these policies was associated with different local needs: the first with the policing, lighting, watching, and cleansing of the town, and the other chiefly with the provision of an adequate jail.

The policing of the town grew more and more inadequate as the town grew in size during the eighteenth century. It rested in the hands of the constables. These were fortified by the compulsory service of the householders at watch and ward under the supervision of the ward constable,[1] service which it often proved difficult to exact,[2] and by such other assistance as the justices thought fit to supply. Even at the time of the municipal reform, after there had been some increase in the police of the town, there were only seventy constables in all, under a salaried chief constable who was paid £50 a year.[3]

Various palliatives were tried by common hall and sessions. In 1688 the common hall appointed a bellman to patrol the streets every night from 10 May to Michaelmas, 'with a bell in his hand to ring as he goes along'. The townspeople were to pay for his giving warning with his bell according to their status in the civic hierarchy.[4] Again, in the summer of 1705 the grand jury desiderated

---

[1] *Records*, II. 292–3; cf. III. 293.

[2] SR. 1690, 1796, two men refusing either to watch or to pay; SR. 1699.

[3] MCR. 1897, 30 constables and headboroughs, 37–40 general constables. MS. Council Minutes, 13 Jan. 1836, for the salary.

[4] HP. xx, at a common hall of 8 May 1688; aldermen pay 1s., common councilmen a different sum, unreadable owing to the document's being worn. The bellman appointed was Thomas Newton, the town crier. Earlier 'bellmen' were criers or ringers, *Records*, I. 339, 369, II. 301, III. 216.

the appointment of two bellmen,[1] and a year the following October two such bellmen were actually appointed and provided with bell and uniform.[2] This last effort, unlike that of 1688, appears to have had permanent results,[3] and the bellmen, who were usually constables also, survived as long as the old corporation as paid servants of the municipality.[4]

Another method was to make more efficient the traditional system of watch and ward. A short-lived attempt was made in 1748–9, apparently in large part as the result of an epidemic of burglaries, when the aldermen of wards were charged to see to the appointment of a nightly watch in their wards, and the watchmen were to be paid a shilling a night out of funds in the hands of the chamberlains.[5] At the following Lady Day the payment was reduced to ninepence.[6] This again was transitory. Other methods were tried spasmodically. Thus in 1770 the corporation erected six street lamps[7] and in 1787 arrangements were made for lighting and watching by private subscription.[8] Again, in 1810, the corporation considered erecting guard-houses or watch-houses in the town.[9] But such spasmodic efforts could effect no improvement. The newly invented gas lighting was of a poor quality,[10] and inhabitants dared not venture out at night. Complaint was made even in the common hall of the senility of the watchmen.[11] The municipal commissioners reported that the town was insufficiently lighted, not regularly watched even in the winter, and never in the summer.[12]

The streets were not merely dark at night, but were also dirty and ill kept. Difficulty was found in securing the most elementary decencies. It was no uncommon thing for householders to be indicted at the sessions for

---

[1] SR. 1705.   [2] HB. 8 Oct. 1706.
[3] References in HB. 25 Sept. 1713, 23 Dec. 1748, 17 Oct. 1769.
[4] MS. Council Minutes, 13 Jan. 1836, 'two bellmen, £10 10s. each, ditto, as constables, £10 each'.
[5] HB. 23 Dec. 1748.   [6] HB. 1 Mar. 1748/9.
[7] HB. 26 Sept. 1770.
[8] Throsby, *History*, 170; Nichols, i. 450.
[9] HB. 9 Mar. 1810.   [10] *Leicester Journal*, 5 Dec. 1823.
[11] HB. 24 Mar. 1829.   [12] MCR. 1897.

'causing obstruction in the King's highway by laying there, and letting lie there for some time, heaps of muck, dung &c.'[1] Stopped-up streams overflowed and caused inconvenience.[2] Carts with iron-bound wheels had to be prevented from breaking up the crude surfaces of the roadways.[3]

The root of the difficulty lay in the highway law, which was substantially unaltered since the Highways Act of Philip and Mary.[4] This made the individual holders of property abutting on the highway responsible for the up-keep of half the roadway at their doors, but when there was doubt about the apportioning of responsibility, or when the efforts of the undoubtedly responsible owners proved not enough, then the parish was held responsible. The surveyor of highways that the parish had to appoint under the acts of 1555 and 1563[5] was thus in as un-enviable a position as the petty constable. He was buffeted about between the householder anxious to evade the four[6] or later six[7] days' statute labour or its commutation, the parish desirous to evade as much repairing work as possi-ble, and the justices who with pains and penalties could compel both surveyor and parish to maintain the streets and roads.

The position of the Leicester corporation under this system is particularly worthy of notice. As the owner of property in the town it was liable exactly as other property-holders to keep its pieces of road in repair.[8] Through those of its members who were justices it was concerned also in the enforcing of the law upon its fellow owners. To it there was also attached a vague responsibility for the general well-being of the town.

It is difficult to separate the public and private capaci ties of the corporation in its dealings with the streets. At times it seems in a public-spirited way to have tried

---

[1] SR. 1709, 1752, 1753, 1772, 1776.
[2] SR. 1709, 1764; HB. 14 Apr. and 10 May 1746.
[3] SR. 1709.　　　　[4] 2 & 3 Philip and Mary, c. 8 (1555).
[5] See *ELG.* v. 14–26.　　　[6] As in 2 & 3 Philip and Mary, c. 8.
[7] As in 5 Eliz. c. 13.
[8] MS. Chamberlains' Books of Payments contain lists of places for which the corporation was responsible.

to keep the streets and approaches of the town in good order. By degrees it built up a staff for this purpose. Already in 1689 it was part of the duty of the beadle to keep those streets swept for which the corporation was responsible.[1] In 1720 the crier was ordered to publish a proclamation of James I for cleansing the streets.[2] There was also, under the supervision of the aldermen of the wards, a scavenging service maintained by a scavengers rate.[3] Moreover, in 1734 the chamberlains had the viewing of the streets and the presenting of encroachments thrust upon them as a regular part of their already too multifarious duties;[4] and in 1786 they were given the assistance of the mace-bearer in this task.[5] Finally, out of the innumerable *ad hoc* committees, a regular pavements committee developed about 1800, the main duty of which was to determine the liability each year of the corporation in street repairs, subject to its not spending more than £150 a year.[6]

But in general we may say that the corporation was like every other property-holder, anxious to shift as much on to others, parishes or individuals, as possible. It is this, rather than disinterested zeal, that often explains the magistrates' activity in inciting constables to search out unsatisfactory pavements or highways, and the readiness of the grand jury of councilmen in presenting offences. In its determination to evade responsibility, where possible, for the streets, two methods were adopted by the corporation.

There was first the straightforward method of litigation. Thus in 1723 there was a dispute with All Saints' parish about ' the road by the meeting house ',[7] which was carried to the assizes, and settled by a division of responsibility

---

[1] CA. *passim.*

[2] HB. 20 Nov. 1720; cf. *Records*, IV. 101, 104, 260.

[3] HB. 18 May 1730, 10 Sept. 1731; for an indication that it was farmed out, HB. 4 Mar. 1761, payment to alderman Ayre of £10 due to him for several years past for scavenging work. There is no evidence to show whether this means the end of the scavenging rate.

[4] HB. 25 Jan. 1733/4.

[5] HB. 22 Sept. 1786; the mace-bearer given extra salary.

[6] HB. 16 Jan. 1800, 8 May 1802.

[7] HB. 19 June 1723.

for the road between the contending parties.[1] In 1795 contention arose about New street, a highly select residential thoroughfare tenanted almost exclusively by members of the corporation, and this dispute was settled in the corporation's favour against S. Martin's parish.[2] The corporation was not so successful in a dispute with S. Margaret's parish about Humberstone gate.[3]

More indirect methods were adopted by a show of great public benevolence. It is not necessary to see this hypocrisy in the co-operation with S. Martin's parish on two occasions in repairing Friar Lane.[4] On the other hand, its grants amounting to £2,500 towards the laying out of new streets where there had formerly been the unenclosed south field of the town, so far from being disinterested and public-spirited contributions to the general welfare, as the corporation wished the municipal commissioners to think, merely served to increase its own revenues.[5] More blatantly self-regarding was the policy adopted in the early part of the nineteenth century of making a mildly generous contribution to present expenditure on the distinct understanding that the parish accepted all future responsibility. Thus in 1826 the corporation decided to pay £100 towards the repair of the Church gate and £50 for Humberstone gate provided that the parish undertook entire charge of these streets for the future.[6]

---

[1] HB. 12 Feb. 1724/5, order for the repair of the corporation's part of the road; cf. 26 July 1745.

[2] *Leicester Herald*, 23 and 30 Jan. 1795; Leicester Cathedral, MS. S. Martin's vestry book, no. 21, 16 Feb., 4 May, 14 May 1795. Presentment ordered to be removed by *certiorari* to King's Bench, 4 May 1802; counsel's opinion that the parish was responsible, 20 July 1802.

[3] Press 24 (4), *The King* v. *Mayor &c. of . . . Leicester*; heard at the county sessions 1779. Lowdham, the corporation's solicitor, protested against the county justices hearing the case. The corporation repaired the road, not being able to prove right instance of any other person's doing it.

[4] HB. 30 Mar. 1725/6; cf. 1 May 1820. Similar co-operation in the Beast Fair, the corporation contributing £20, on condition that the parishes of S. Martin and S. Margaret found the rest; HB. 2 Sept. 1794.

[5] HB. 5 Aug. 1806, 'in the Bowling Green and Smart's close'; HB. 3 Mar. 1807, in the Bowling Green garden; also HB. 5 Aug. 1808, for street, to be flagged, between the High street and Freeschool lane, a grant of fifty guineas. MCR. 1906, sums amounting to £2,502 1s. spent in this way, out of funds raised by sale of land in the south field.

[6] HB. 16 Mar. 1826; S. Margaret's vestry, MS. Minutes, 12 and 27 Apr. 1826.

The third of the needs of the town associated with the
projects of a local act does not bring out the impossibility
of the old lack of system in such high relief. The water-
supply came from two sources, the conduit and the wells,
from which it was taken by water-carriers, at the price of
a halfpenny a bucket, to the kitchen.[1] The conduit, which
had been erected in the seventeenth century,[2] was an archi-
tectural embellishment to the Saturday market-place. It
brought water from fresh springs outside the town in
S. Margaret's field. The Inclosure Act of 1764 for S.
Margaret's field prohibited the digging of wells within
fifty yards of the culvert,[3] a provision which was sometimes disobeyed and disobedience punished.[4] In the early
part of our period the corporation concerned itself with
the repair of the conduit,[5] and in 1709 handsomely rebuilt
it at a more convenient site.[6] Later the corporation's
interest in the conduit became less generous. So in 1771
it was at their own expense, not the corporation's, that
the inhabitants were allowed to build a cistern under the
pavement to receive waste water from the conduit.[7] By
the nineteenth century this ornament was a nuisance. In
1825 users of the market-place petitioned for its removal,[8]
as a source of obstruction, but it was not finally pulled
down till the middle of the century,[9] its place being taken
by a statue of a duke of Rutland.[10]

The wells were an interesting feature of the town's life.
They were maintained through the wards by a rate, apparently like the constable's rate, based on land occupied
by the ratepayer.[11] Unlike the conduit, they were never
the general responsibility of the corporation, which only

[1] R. Read, *Modern Leicester* (1881), 27.

[2] Throsby, *History*, 376; Nichols, i. 441,486 n.,533; C. J. Billson, *Mediaeva
Leicester* (1920), cf. 11 with 207.

[3] Statute 4 Geo. III (private), no. 14, p. 14.

[4] *Leicester Journal*, 9 July 1824, 18 Mar. 1825; HB. 30 Aug. 1825.

[5] HB. 31 Mar. 1697; Nichols, i. 318 n., 441, 439.

[6] HB. 10 and 13 June 1709.

[7] HB. 26 July 1771; Nichols, i. 533.

[8] HB. 30 Aug. 1825, petition referred to the market-place committee.

[9] J. Storey, *Historical Sketch 1836–93* (1895), 104–5.

[10] This statue was subsequently removed.

[11] e.g. MS. S. Martin's vestry minutes contain notes of regular payment for
well rate; cf. Nichols, i. 591.

concerned itself with those on its own land.[1] Each ward
had two well-reeves,[2] and for special reasons individuals
might be singled out to maintain particular wells.[3] There
were the usual difficulties: householders were dilatory in
their contributions to the cost of setting pumps in the
wells,[4] and in 1716 the well-reeves and inhabitants of a
ward were collectively indicted for neglect.[5] There were
also the usual difficulties in fixing responsibility for maintenance.[6] It appears to have been with a view to strengthening the hand of the justices that the only by-law recorded
in our period as having received the sanction of the justices
in assize was passed in 1759. This authorized the setting
of pumps in all the wells that had from time immemorial
stood for public use in the streets of Leicester; provided
for the appointment of two pump-reeves in each ward,
and for the levying by them of a pump rate, charged on
the same basis as the land-tax assessments, and levied in
the same way as the poor rate.[7]

On two occasions only, so far as can be ascertained
from the records available, did the corporation make any
serious attempt at a radical reform in these essential
services, namely in 1749–50 and in 1822. The first of
these attempts was made at a time when the corporation
of Leicester was under the influence of that wave of urban
improvement that flourished in the middle years of the
eighteenth century.[8] This attempt to obtain a local act
came during a difficult winter and was prompted by an
epidemic of burglaries. The corporation supported the
claim by reference to the deplorable state of the Leicester
streets, which it ascribed to its not possessing adequate

---

[1] e.g. HB. 15 May 1723, order for pump to be set in the schoolhouse yard
'where the well now is'; HB. 18 July 1718, permission for a tenant to lay
a lead pipe from chapel-well to horse-trough.

[2] HB. 4 Dec. 1717, a very unusual entry of the swearing in of well-reeves.

[3] SR. 1706, the well at the Gainsborough was in a dangerous state, and four
persons were chosen as well-reeves.   HP. xxi, common hall, 12 Apr. 1706, grant
of £3 for setting down a pump at the Gainsborough well.

[4] SR. 1713.   [5] SR. 1716.

[6] HB. 5 Feb. 1723/4.

[7] HB. 22 Nov. 1759; for the method of assessment, cf. E. Cannan, *History of
Local Rates in England* (1927), 114–19, 129–30.

[8] Cf. Thompson, 79; M. C. Buer, *Health, Wealth, and Population 1760–1815*
(1926), 40, 59–62, 76–88.

rating powers.[1] For whatever reason—possibly the prevalent distrust of rating faculties had some influence [2]—
the attempt was abortive, and the town reverted for three-
quarters of a century to the fruitless pursuit of ineffective
expedients.

The next serious effort came when the growth of the
town had made conditions infinitely worse, and opposition
to the corporation was, as we shall see, bitter and organized.[3] The plan of 1822 for a local improvement act for
Leicester, similar to those obtained for the great majority
of English towns, failed chiefly because, only in the previous year, there had been set up by act of parliament a
gas, light, and coke company, of which all the directors
were identified with the opposition to the corporation,[4]
and amongst the original shareholders of which were
members of the corporation.[5] Consequently, since the
interests of the gas company were apparently threatened
by the new scheme, there was open division in the common hall. The corporation was not united in support of
the project, and its own committee concluded 'that any
legislative measure for this purpose is unnecessary'.[6]

The local radicals were, on the other hand, united in
condemnation of the plan for a local act. They held that
the plan was too expensive in proportion to the good that
it would do.[7] In addition, they maintained that for such
a public purpose so wealthy a corporation as that of
Leicester should use its corporate funds. At the public
meeting, held by the mayor, in consequence of an influential petition supported by prominent shareholders of
the gas company as well as by members of the corporation,[8]

---

[1] HB. 1 Dec. 1749; HCJ. xx. 927–8 (15 Jan. 1749/50), 941; Nichols, i. 440;
Thompson, 79. The argument about rates was probably a mere excuse, as the
justices had adequate powers of coercion, at least in some parts of their field, had
they cared to use them; ELG. v. 21–4.

[2] Cf. ELG. i. 246.   [3] See below, pp. 115 ff.

[4] Names in J. Storey, *Historical Sketch* (1895), 92.

[5] Statute 1 & 2 Geo. IV, c. iii (Local and personal, declared public); I count
7 members of the common hall out of 69 original proprietors.

[6] HB. 16 Jan. 1822.

[7] Allowing for existing provision, £3,000 for 50 extra men and lamps.

[8] HB. ibid., 39 petitioners, 16 shareholders, 7 corporators.

the radicals not merely condemned the plan that they had met to discuss, but took the chance of denouncing the corporate system root and branch.[1] The improvement plan was killed by party hate and by private enterprise. A later effort of 1831 made even less progress.[2]

The lighting of the Leicester streets remained still, therefore, a matter of private subscriptions, the corporation participating.[3] In 1831–2 three of the town parishes, S. Martin's, S. Margaret's, and S. Mary's, under the act of 1830[4] made their own arrangements for lighting and watching.[5] Leicester thus remained as one of the only four considerably large municipal towns without improvement commissioners,[6] necessary though these were.

Those critics of the 1822 plan that demanded that corporate funds should be applied to public, rather than to merely corporation, projects raised a most fundamental issue.[7] For the corporation did not interpret the public responsibilities placed upon it by the charter as meaning that its funds should be applicable to any and every public purpose. On its interpretation, corporate revenues were to be used for corporate purposes, just as college revenues might be used for college purposes.[8] The justices probably also argued that the objectors wanted public improvement without being willing to pay for it, and that the wealth of the corporation was grossly exaggerated by the radical party,[9] just as the wealth of the established church was.[10] Further, another line of objection was taken by a party in the corporation, to the effect that a rate would fall equally on rich and poor, but not equitably according to the amount of protection given by better lighting of the streets,

[1] HB. 16 Jan., 1 Feb. 1822; *Leicester Journal,* 21 Dec. 1821, 25 Jan. 1822, 8 Feb. 1822; *ELG.* iv. 302–3.

[2] HB. 5 Sept. 1831.   [3] HB. 29 Mar. 1832.

[4] Statute 11 Geo. IV and 1 Will. IV, c. 27; repealed by 3 & 4 Will. IV, c. 90, 1.

[5] Leicester Cathedral, MS. S. Martin's vestry book, 20 Dec. 1831; HB. 27 Aug. 1832; S. Margaret's MS. Vestry Book, 29 Dec. 1831; *ELG.* iv. 310; G. R. Searson, *Twenty-five Years of Liberalism in Leicester* (Leicester, 1872), 29.

[6] *ELG.* iv. 242 n. 2.   [7] *ELG.* iii. 733–6.

[8] Cf. Observations of Thomas Burbidge cited below, pp. 85, 126.

[9] The corporation was vastly in debt at its dissolution, although its income was considerable, see below, pp. 139–40.

[10] W. L. Mathieson, *English Church Reform 1815–40* (1923), 25.

and that therefore the 'watching and lighting of the town ought to be borne by the wealthier part of the Inhabitants *exclusively*'.[1] This doctrine can hardly have pleased those wealthy manufacturers who were among the corporation's opponents, especially as the project was expensive to a degree. It was, moreover, a doctrine that the magistrates were disposed to work upon in the administration of the poor law.[2] Indeed, there was ground for distrusting any plan that might increase the rating power of the justices, either by putting more power in the hands of the corporation, or more indirectly, in the hands of a body of improvement commissioners that the justices might dominate.

The alternative means adopted by the justices in their persistent desire for more adequate rating authority was legal rather than legislative. It involved the town's need of a commodious prison. More important, it raised difficult questions of the magistrates' jurisdiction. In its outcome it was even more decisive in consequences for the government of the town than the failure to obtain a local act.

The various statutory rates already levied in the town, and the scavenging and well rates, continued to be levied in spite of the rebuff of 1750, and formed the basis of the next attempt of the town magistracy. The justices, by virtue of their office, enjoyed the power to levy a rate of the nature of a county rate, that is, roughly speaking, a rate consolidating these existing various rates for particular objects. This power was confirmed to them by two acts of George II.[3] The weakness of the Leicester magistrates' position lay in that the area of their jurisdiction was doubtful—which may explain their having first adopted the more circuitous procedure of the local act. For it was not certain whether the borough magistrates' jurisdiction extended beyond the confines of the borough proper, to include the liberties.

This was an ancient problem, and may for its ultimate origin be traced back to the relations established between

---

[1] HB. 16 Jan. 1822.　　　　[2] *ELG.* i. 589–96.
[3] E. Cannan, op. cit. 109–10. Statutes 12 Geo. II, c. 29, 'for the more easy assessing collecting and levying of county rates', and 13 Geo. II, c. 18, in part 'for extending the powers and authorities of Justices of the Peace of Counties, touching County rates, to the Justices of the Peace of such Liberties and Franchises as have Commissions of Peace within themselves'.

the medieval borough and the manorial jurisdictions impingeing on it, of which the liberties were relics.[1] The charter of 1599 was ambiguous as to the degree of control enjoyed by the justices in the Bishop's Fee and other liberties,[2] and early in the reign of James I the corporation made an attempt to clarify the position in its own interest.[3] By the middle of the eighteenth century this problem was far more than merely academic or ancient. It was urgent. For now the population of the town was growing, and more of its inhabitants resided in the liberties. Thus, on rating grounds alone, the justices had strong reasons for establishing their jurisdiction in the liberties of the Bishop's Fee, the Castle view, Wood gate, the Newarke, and Bromkinsthorpe. It was simply that the borough justices aimed at making their exclusive jurisdiction coterminous with the town.

Until 1765 the borough justices suffered the exercise in the liberties of jurisdiction by the county magistrates.[4] The county then sought legal advice, and obtained counsel's opinion from no less an authority than Charles Yorke, the distinguished son of the great Lord Hardwicke. Yorke's advice was that, on the wording of the charters, especially that of 1599, the borough had sole jurisdiction in the liberties to the total exclusion of the county.[5] This opinion led to the county magistrates' withdrawal.[6]

[1] *Records*, I. xvii–xxii, liii–liv; cf. C. Gross, *The Gild Merchant* (1890), i. 56, 68, ii. 140, 141; the bishop of Lincoln's tenants in the Bishop's Fee were allowed to become gildsmen, but not thereby burgesses.

[2] Nichols, i, Appendix, 414; *Records*, III. 359 ff., in abridging the charter omits some of the phrases of importance in this case. Crucial words are: town J.P.s 'tam ad pacem in eodem burgo ac libertatibus et praecinctis eiusdem conservandum'; mayor, &c. 'deinceps in perpetuum habeant . . . omnibus & singulis eisdem consimilibus juribus, libertatibus [etc.] . . . jurisdicionibus in omnibus & singulis eisdem parochiis S. Margaretae S. Mariae S. Leonardi et le Newarke, qualia et quae, *ac in tam amplis modo & forma* prout iidem major ballivi & burgenses virtute harum literarum . . . patentium aut aliorum progenitorum nostrorum habere uti et gaudere possint aut debent in praedicto burgo de Leicester aut in aliquo membro vel parte vel parcella eiusdem burgi'; *saving* rights of Crown, and *all other rights granted to any other persons or bodies corporate*, 'aliter quam praedictis majori ballivis [etc.] . . . concessis'.

[3] *Records*, IV. xxvii–xxviii, 18–19; cf. 96.

[4] They enjoyed certain rights of billeting soldiers (papers in *Davis* v. *Nedham*), and in the Bishop's Fee also of inspecting weights and measures (papers in *Blankley* v. *Winstanley*).

[5] Opinion of C. Yorke, dated 21 Aug. 1766.

[6] Press 5; case for the plaintiff in *Blankley* v. *Winstanley*.

At the same time, the justices took advantage of this ruling to appoint, as they could under the important county rate legislation of 1739–40, a borough treasurer, and to arrange for the collection by the borough chief constable of a general borough rate, from the officers of the various parishes and the constable of the Newarke out of the poor levies raised by them. In practice, this rate was ordered 'not by the borough justices at the sessions—only by verbal order or warrant to the chief constable out of sessions '.[1] They began also to appoint constables in all the liberties,[2] and to behave there exactly as in the rest of the town.

The common hall gave much attention to this campaign and indemnified its officers in case of actions being brought against them in their execution of this expansionist policy.[3] The corporation's zeal took in November 1766 a spectacular form. Since 1609 it had been the duty of the newly elected mayor soon after his election to go to the castle, there to make oath to safeguard the rights in the borough of the duchy of Lancaster.[4] In token of submission the town mace had been sloped at the entry to the castle view.[5] In 1766 and again in 1767 the sloping of the mace was refused. The first time the steward of the duchy, Thomas Pares senior, was absent, and represented by his son,[6] who allowed the innovation to pass, so that the mayor, alderman

---

[1] Press 5 ; case against the county in *Davis* v. *Nedham.* The statutes were of considerable practical importance and were cited also in the case of *Bates* v. *Winstanley* in 1815, on which see below, p. 39; 12 Geo. II, c. 29, 'an act for the more easy assessing and levying of county rates ', see especially §§ 6, 7 ; 13 Geo. II, c. 18, amongst other things, removed doubt by extending the provisions of 12 Geo. II, c. 29, to all places in England, not being counties, that had quarter sessions. Cf. *ELG.* ii. 389, which speaks of borough magistrates as levying a rate on their own authority, ' in imitation of the justices of the county '.

[2] They had been used to appoint a constable for the Bishop's Fee, but 'never required any duty from him nor did he exercise any ' ; in the Bishop's Fee, Braunstone gate, and Wood gate constables were appointed by the county ; in the Newarke, which was extra-parochial, there were no officers ; the constabulary of the castle was appointed by letters patent from the Crown.

[3] HB. 26 Apr. 1765, 18 Oct. 1765, 25 Mar. 1767 ; on this last occasion the hall ' upon good advice adjudged that the castle view is in the borough jurisdiction '.

[4] *Records*, IV. xxix. 85 ; HP. xx, fo. 182.   [5] *Records*, IV. 95–6.

[6] Thomas Pares, M.P., who plays a considerable part in the political life of the town, 1818–26, was the grandson of the steward.

Fisher, was sworn. The second time the mayor, alderman Holmes, was met by the firm refusal of Pares senior to permit entry to the castle unless the traditional ritual of deference was followed. In consequence the oath was not again taken till 1768, when the town clerk and Pares agreed that it be taken privately. The reason for the steward's firmness is significant, namely that the mace must be sloped, because the castle was outside the borough jurisdiction.[1] Thus the real point of the incidents of 1766 and 1767 lies in the borough magistrates' policy of establishing control in the liberties.[2]

Within five years the county magistrates took up the challenge. The first two attempts to bring the matter to a decisive issue came to nothing.[3] At last a final decision was obtained in the case of *Blankley* v. *Winstanley*. Blankley was an apprentice of the Bishop's Fee who had disobeyed his master's lawful command and was therefore arrested by a warrant from two county justices, Winstanley and Burnaby, to be by them committed to hard labour in the county house of correction. The issue was the clearer because neither master nor apprentice was free of the borough. The corporation immediately took this up as a test case.[4] It was argued in King's Bench, on the wording of the charters and previous usage. Judgement was given in 1789 against the corporation. Chiefly on the ground that there were no words in the charter expressly excluding the county justices from the Bishop's Fee, and like areas, and since there was no long usage to support the corporation's reading of an ambiguous text, jurisdiction in the liberties was declared to be concurrent.[5] So it remained till the end of the old corporation's life.[6]

---

[1] PRO. DL 41/92, affidavit of John Heyrick (town clerk 1764–91) in a case of 1806. According to Heyrick the refusal to slope the mace had the active encouragement of William Burleton (recorder 1766–87); indeed was inspired by him.

[2] Leicester historians have been prone to ascribe the refusal to alderman Fisher's jacobitism; so Thompson, 130: this view is not expressed by Throsby, *History*, 163.

[3] On technical grounds in 1771 (*Davis* v. *Nedham*); and in 1775–9 (*Throsby* v. *Bunney*) both parties agreed not to raise the question. Press 5.

[4] HB. 24 Nov. 1786.

[5] Press 2; Nichols, i. 567; C. Durnford and E. H. East, *Reports of Cases in the King's Bench*, iii (1790), 279–86, full summary of arguments.

[6] MCR. 1889.

Jurisdiction being shared, the important power of levying a rate was as regarded the liberties in doubt. This was settled in 1815 by King's Bench, in a case that arose out of the action of S. Mary's parish in joining with the borough justices to contest the levying of a rate on the south field by the county magistrates.[1] Judgement was given against the corporation, to the effect that the liberties paid to the county. In consequence the general borough rate fell exclusively on the restricted area of the borough, although this contained a diminishing proportion of the town's inhabitants.

Even the solitary success of the magistrates in increasing their rating powers by the obtaining of a jail rate only increased the difficulty. One of the objects contemplated by the justices when they started on their campaign to secure powers of taxation in the liberties was the jail. In 1769,[2] and again (after Howard's visit in 1787 to Leicester)[3] in 1791, the grand jury presented at the sessions that the jail was ruinous and unsafe.[4] Two purposes were served by these presentments of the grand jury. First, the justices complied with the act of 1739 which made presentment by the grand jury a necessary preliminary of expenditure on jails, bridges, and houses of correction.[5] Second, the jury announced what was to be the policy of the justices, who dominated the corporation, from which the jury was exclusively recruited. For, whereas in the past the town jail had been maintained out of funds administered by the common hall, now for the future the cost of its upkeep was to be borne by the inhabitants at large. This meant of course only those within the town magistrates' jurisdiction. This policy being announced, a new jail was built according to the ideas of Howard.[6] The Leicester corporation was one of the few corporations that took any notice of Howard's criticisms.[7]

[1] HB. 29 July 1811; MCR. 1898; Maule and Selwyn, *Reports of Cases in King's Bench 1816–17* (1817), 429–37, case of *Bates v. Winstanley and another*, especially 435, for the judgement of Ellenborough C.J.

[2] SR., Box 1769–72, dated 2 Oct. 1769.

[3] Gardiner, *Music and Friends*, i (1838), 71–3; Thompson, 184; *Leicester Journal*, 3 Nov. 1787.

[4] Ibid., 9 Dec. 1791.

[5] Statute 12 Geo. II, c. 29; *ELG.* i. 450–1.

[6] Thompson, 199.   [7] *ELG.* vi. 63 n. 3.

The principle that the inhabitants, and not the corporation, were responsible for the jail was underlined in 1823 by the important act consolidating the prison law, a portion of an extended scheme of Peelite reform.[1] This act mentioned among seventeen prisons to be repaired that of Leicester. It authorized the justices to levy a special rate for this purpose.[2] The act gave much umbrage to the local radical critics of the close corporation. These alleged that the corporation had put pressure on the government to secure the inclusion of Leicester in the act so as definitively to thrust the care of the jail on to the inhabitants.[3] Further, the magistrates incurred an immense debt on the rebuilding and enlarging of the jail by accepting an outrageous tender from one of its own senior members.[4] Moreover, this expense, of some £4,000 on land for a new jail, was at least in part wasted. For when the county in 1828 erected on corporation land in the old south field[5] a new jail, a pretentious neo-Gothic fortress derided by Cobbett,[6] the town justices took over and rebuilt the old county jail[7] and abandoned their original project.

The new jail rate was from the outset unpopular. Petitioners to the commons complained of the unfairness of the town's having to keep a jail, 'when a great part of the town called the Bishop's Fee is situated in the county'.[8] Discontent at the new rate reinforced discontent at the borough rate levied since 1766. In 1824 the opposition, led by members of S. Martin's vestry,[9] obtained a mandamus from King's Bench to inspect the accounts of the borough rates, of which only the most jejune summary was

---

[1] *ELG.* vi. 74–5 ; statute 4 Geo. IV, c. 64 ; see schedule A.

[2] *ELG.* vi. 75 n. 3.

[3] *Leicester Journal,* 18 July 1828.

[4] MCR. 1920–1 : the contractor was alderman Firmadge, 'architect'.

[5] The present jail for the town and county on the Welford road : see J. Storey, op. cit. 46 ; cf. Fielding Johnson, *Glimpses of Ancient Leicester* (1906), 302.

[6] W. Cobbett, *Rural Rides,* ed. G. D. H. and M. Cole (1930), 663.

[7] Thompson, 199 ; MCR. 1897–8.

[8] *HCJ.* lxxix. 205, *Leicester Journal,* 19 Mar. 1824.

[9] Leicester Cathedral, MS. S. Martin's vestry book, no. 21, Apr. 1824 (four meetings) ; the Pagets and other liberal leaders in the town lived in S. Martin's parish. S. Nicholas' and All Saints' also took part. *Leicester Journal,* 23 Apr., 7 May 1824.

published.[1] Certain criticisms were made, but as yet opposition was not pressed.[2] In 1827 the critics, again more aggressive, sought from King's Bench a condemnation of the expenditure, which the justices had made, of £1,343 on special constables in the election of 1826, but the court upheld the magistrates.[3] The critics also kept their objections before the house of commons.[4] The justices, on the other hand, argued that they had put off expense as long as possible, that their motive in borrowing for the jail had been to save the rates, and that they sent as many prisoners as they could to the county jail for offences which had been committed in the liberties, as they now could under a ruling of King's Bench in 1826.[5]

Thus, even when allowance has been made for the extravagance and selfishness of the unreformed corporation,[6] the defeat of the justices in their attempt to assert their jurisdiction in the liberties is of even more crucial importance than the failure to obtain a local act, in accounting for the misgovernment of Leicester in the first three and a half decades of the nineteenth century. More than this, it was a factor in the political bitterness that made these years in some ways so hectic.[7] It no doubt contributed to the growing reluctance of the magistracy to do anything that might conceivably be thrust on to any other authority. For the adverse judgements of 1789 and 1815 perpetuated a 'glaring maladjustment of jurisdictions and areas'.[8] Indeed, they aggravated this maladjustment. The town rates fell heavily on the comparatively few residents in the borough jurisdiction, so that to avoid the heavy rate there was a continual migration 'from the old borough to the new', the example being set by a majority of the corporation.[9]

[1] Ibid., e.g. 7 May 1824, 2 Dec. 1825.
[2] Leicester Cathedral, loc. cit., 8 and 22 Apr.; *Leicester Journal*, 21 Apr. 1826. Probably the affair was not pressed in view of the approaching election.
[3] Ibid., 22 June; *Leicester Chronicle*, 10 Feb., 12 May 1827; cf. *Leicester Journal*, 30 May 1828.
[4] e.g. ibid., 28 Mar., 27 June, 18 July 1828.
[5] Ibid., 23 May 1828; MCR. 1897; Hansard, N.S. xix. 1762; *Leicester Chronicle*, 24 Feb. 1827.
[6] See below, pp. 139–40.　　　　　[7] See below, pp. 115 ff.
[8] *ELG*. iii. 722, cf. ii. 288–92.　　　　　[9] MCR. 1920.

There is yet another field in which we can observe the break-down of the Elisabethan system, with its concentration of power in the hands of the justices, namely the poor law. Here more than anywhere else we find hostility between the bench and the parishes. Here, as with the improving of the town, we find attempts to escape from the difficulties of an obsolete system.

From time to time during the eighteenth century attempts were made to form a union of the Leicester parishes, so that the town might become for the purposes of poor-law administration, as the justices desired it to be for rating, one unit. The first attempt was made in 1708, when in consequence of the Bristol experiment the workhouse movement was spreading rapidly over the country.[1] The corporation energetically furthered the progress through the house of commons of a bill for the town workhouse, under six guardians, representing the union of the six parishes, for the purposes of employing the poor, bringing them up in 'Principalls of good religion', and as well securing 'advantage to all the Parishes in the Corporation in respect of the charges they now pay to the Poor'.[2] At first the scheme prospered,[3] but in the end, like all the other schemes that involved the levying of a town rate, it proved abortive.[4] Consequently Leicester remained with only its parish houses.[5]

The consequences of a tradition of parochialism were seen in the failure of a further attempt nearly ninety years later. In 1792 it was suggested, apparently by a radical dissenter, that a workhouse on the Shrewsbury plan should be set up in Leicester.[6] In spite of its nonconformist origin, the project had the influential support of clergy and gentry and was congenial to the corporation.[7] After

---

[1] *ELG.* vii. 120–1, 151, 24 n.; G. N. Clark, op. cit. 51–2.

[2] HP. xxi, common hall, 30 Jan. 1707/8; HB. 30 Jan. 1707/8; HP. xxi, an undated paper noting amendments to the bill.

[3] *HCJ.* xv. 529, 546, 593, 609.   [4] Thompson, 22–3.

[5] *Account of Several Workhouses* (1725–32), 88–101; Nichols, i. 556, 585 n., 590 n.; Marshall, op. cit. 110, 130, 146.

[6] *Leicester Journal,* 17 Feb. 1792; suggested by R. B., who is, I suggest, Robert Brewin, a prominent dissenting manufacturer.

[7] Ibid., 24 Feb., 8 Mar. 1792; the mayor was chairman of the committee for the project.

twelve years of propaganda, and an energetic campaign initiated in 1804 by S. Martin's vestry,[1] the project was defeated by the self-satisfied abstention of S. Margaret's vestry, on the ground that, as its own finances were satisfactory, it would lose rather than gain by co-operating with the other parishes.[2] A revival of the plan in 1810 came to nothing. Again its failure was due to the action of S. Margaret's vestry, which now erected a new workhouse for its own use, the existing building being 'very ruinous'.[3]

In consequence of the failure of these poor-law union projects, there was now no poor-law authority standing between magistracy and parishes, nor was there any institution that might be used, like the incorporated guardians of certain towns, as a means of checking the powers of the magistracy. It is also worth noticing that it was the magistracy that took the constructive line, and the parish of S. Margaret's that maintained an obstructive particularism.

Yet in general the Leicester justices had the faults common to their calling. They showed a marked tendency to trouble themselves as little as possible, while at times interfering officiously. The passing of the overseers' accounts, ordered by the poor-law code,[4] became as commonly elsewhere[5] a formality. It was stated in 1811 that S. Martin's accounts had not been made up in proper form for three years, although nominally inspected by the justices.[6] Indolence will also account for the suspicious uniformity with which the magistrates granted petitions from aggrieved parishioners whose allowances had been reduced by the parish officers.[7] There is evidence that the Leicester parishes lived in a state of perpetual warfare against the vicarious generosity of the justices. In 1703 Mary Liggins

---

[1] Leicester Cathedral, MS. S. Martin's vestry book, no. 21, 3 and 13 July 1804; a large committee was appointed of members of both the local political factions.

[2] *Leicester Journal*, 27 July 1804.

[3] S. Margaret's MS. vestry book, 9 Aug. 1810; *Leicester Journal*, 10 Aug. 1810.

[4] 43 Eliz. c. 2.   [5] Marshall, op. cit. 58.

[6] *Leicester Journal*, 15 Oct. 1811.   [7] MCR. 1917.

stated, in petitioning for an increase to her dole, that an officer of S. Mary's parish had declared that 'the Recorders word or order of Sessions signifies nothing'.[1] In 1702 S. Margaret's parish was summoned,[2] and in 1824 the overseers of All Saints' parish were fined,[3] for disobeying the orders of the sessions for the relief of paupers. Such orders were frequent, and disobedience was common. There was continuous litigation about settlements. Yet, with all its experience of friction, waste, and inconvenience, the corporation opposed in 1822 Scarlett's bill for amending the settlement law.[4]

The point chiefly at issue between the justices and the parishes was the control of the parish officers, especially of the overseers, who had great authority and influence.[5] About this issue, the battle was fought for parochial independence. When attempts to organize the poor-law administration of Leicester as one whole had failed, there was only one alternative line of improvement. This was to secure the freedom of the individual parishes from vexatious interference by magistrates. Only in two of the Leicester parishes can we follow the course of this battle with any certainty.

In the large central parish of S. Martin the first steps to gain for the parish more effective control of its poor-law officers were taken in the seventeen-twenties, in the building of a workhouse[6] and the appointment of a workhouse master.[7] The workhouse master came soon to be appointed on clearly defined terms as a salaried officer of the parish, in spite of the doubtful legality of the act,[8] 'chosen overseer to assist the overseers'.[9] In 1797 another method was tried in the appointment by the vestry of a committee of inhabitants to assist the officers.[10] Finally, in 1812, in a large

---

[1] SR. 1703.   [2] SR. 1702.   [3] *Leicester Journal,* 14 May 1824.
[4] HB. 22 May 1822; *ELG.* viii. 346–7.   [5] Marshall, op. cit. 89.
[6] Leicester Cathedral, MS. S. Martin's vestry book, no. 19, 13 Jan. 1720/1, 8 Jan. 1723/4; Nichols, i. 568, 585 n. 2.
[7] Leicester Cathedral, loc. cit., 8 and 18 Jan. 1724/5.
[8] Holdsworth in Dowdell, op. cit. li, quoting an opinion of Lord Mansfield in 1785; such appointments were legalized by 59 Geo. III, c. 12, § 7.
[9] Leicester Cathedral, loc. cit., no. 20, 1 Apr. 1755; the parish experimented a great deal with different types of agreement. Cf. *ELG.* vii. 216–45, 286–7.
[10] Leicester Cathedral, loc. cit., no. 21, 3 May 1797.

and representative meeting, with the approval of both whig and tory partisans, the parish adopted Gilbert's act,[1] so far as this made provision for the internal organization of individual parishes, by the subjecting of its poor-law administration to a committee of guardians, a visitor, and a treasurer.[2]

S. Margaret's parish went much farther in its war with the justices and in the end virtually excluded them from any effective part in its affairs. Pauperism in this parish was by the beginning of the nineteenth century a particularly serious problem,[3] no doubt largely in consequence of the growth of the ' new borough'. The control of the workhouse, first erected in 1714,[4] was thus an urgent matter. For this end, the parish sought in 1800 the magistrates' consent to the appointment of a permanent salaried overseer.[5] This officer's conduct was closely regulated by the vestry, no doubt the more so since there was frequent necessity for protest against the overseers appointed by the justices.[6] A next step was taken in the adoption of the vestry act of 1819, a course taken also by All Saints' and S. Mary's parishes[7] as a means of increasing parish control of parish finance.

The act of 1819 was certainly not enough, for relations with the justices were merely exacerbated, while the officers were still not sufficiently under the control of the vestry. In 1828 one of the overseers, James Rawson, a member of the corporation, quarrelled with the parish, as a result

---

[1] Statute 22 Geo. III, c. 83.
[2] Leicester Cathedral, loc. cit., 13 July 1812.
[3] See H. of C., reports of committees, *Parliamentary Papers*, 1819 (V), 49, select committee on the framework knitters of the town and county of Leicester; account given by Mr. Decimus Cooke of the poor levies of S. Margaret's, Leicester, which reached £7,243 8s. 11d. in 1816, and in the lowest year between 1809 and 1818, viz. 1810, the large sum of £3,540 7s. 11d.
[4] Nichols, i. 556.
[5] S. Margaret's vestry minutes, 15 Apr. 1800, 2 May 1803; also for the discussion of a similar policy by S. Martin's parish, and the decision to keep to the old system of annual appointment, see Leicester Cathedral, loc. cit., no. 21, 8 Apr. 1806.
[6] *ELG.* i. 158–9, 165.
[7] *ELG.* loc. cit.; MCR. 1918; Reports of Commissioners 1834, *Parliamentary Papers*, xxxv, Poor Law Commission's Report, App. B. ii, part i, p. 78, for a criticism of S. Mary's select vestry, question 5.

of his fraudulently profiting out of the furnishing of the
new church of S. George the martyr erected in the parish.[1]
The next year the vestry felt bound to protest against 'the
unusual course of verifying and swearing to accounts before
two magistrates as being correct, without having been
previously examined and signed by the vestry'.[2] In the
following year unusual difficulties were experienced in
collecting the poor rate.[3]

It is obvious that the justices encouraged overseers to
circumvent the vestry. Finally, therefore, it was decided
to apply to parliament for a local act for the parish as
a last weapon against the bench.[4] After much arguing,[5]
and in spite of the virulent opposition of Burbidge, acting
for the justices,[6] S. Margaret's parish got its select vestry
act.[7] The final provisions were a compromise between the
contending parties, but a compromise favouring the parish.
Parish affairs were to be conducted by a committee of
management, or select vestry, consisting of the vicar and
officers of the parish, with twenty ratepayers elected by
the inhabitants in vestry assembled, the franchise being
determined by a fairly low property qualification.[8] The
officers were to be chosen by the magistrates from lists
submitted by the vestry. The really vital clause in the act
provided that 'in all things relating to the care and management of the poor, or the affairs of the said parish', the
officers were 'under the control and direction of the said
vestry'.[9] It was a final defeat for the magistracy. At last
one parish had gained adequate control of its officers and

---

[1] *Leicester Journal*, 13 and 20 June, 1 Aug. 1828. The erection of
S. George's church is itself evidence of the growth of population in this parish.
The corporation gave 200 guineas to the erection of the church, attended the
stone-laying in state, and granted an annuity of £10 to the organist, similar to
annuities to other organists in the town, HB. 26 Aug. 1819, 6 Aug. 1823,
1 Apr. 1833.

[2] S. Margaret's, loc. cit., 3 Aug. 1829; cf. *ELG*. i. 119 n. 3.

[3] S. Margaret's, loc. cit., 2 Nov. 1829, 12 July 1830.

[4] Ibid., 2 June 1831.   [5] Ibid., 1831–2.

[6] G. R. Searson, *Twenty-five Years*, 28–9; MCR. 1918; *HCJ*. lxxxvii. 106,
hostile petition from the corporation of Leicester, and another from the sur-
veyors of the highways.

[7] Statute 2 Will. IV (local and personal, declared public), c. x.

[8] Clause 12.

[9] Clause 31; MCR. 1899.

adequate independence of the justices. By April 1834 it was out of debt, and a revaluation was undertaken.[1]

Yet the town as a whole laboured under a great burden of pauperism, and the adoption of select vestries in other parishes than S. Margaret's brought no improvement for more than a short time.[2] The poor-law commissioners, while refraining from a detailed examination of circumstances in Leicester, anticipated that the poor-law rate in the town would rise rather than fall, and declared that 'if not checked by the timely interference of the legislature, this dreadful evil threatens at no very distant time to paralyse the industry and swallow up the property of the whole town'.[3] Legislative interference was soon to come. Municipal corporations and the poor-law system were within no very distant time entirely remodelled. The determination of the middle classes to economize, that had in Leicester its part in the effective resistance of S. Margaret's vestry, began to create its Bumbledom over the larger part of the country.

The local act for S. Margaret's vestry aptly closes our survey of the justices' failure to provide in Leicester a necessary minimum of social services. It does not appear that either they or their opponents are exclusively to blame, though there was obstinacy on the one side, factiousness on the other. The hostility to them engendered by their dealings with the parishes was therefore all the more increased by their efforts to secure adequate rating powers. It is a significant fact that the municipal reform of 1835 corrected the maladjustment of jurisdiction and area, while it vested in the new corporations powers of lighting and watching, with power also to levy a borough rate.[4]

[1] S. Margaret's, loc. cit., 22 Mar. 1834, a printed report.
[2] Cf. Poor Law Commission Report (1834), App. B. i, part iv, pp. 78 f., the answers from S. Mary's parish, Leicester, that the parish had had a select vestry as provided by 59 Geo. III, c. 12, for the last twelve years. 'Its effect when first established was good, but during the last five or six years they have arrogated so much power to themselves that they have become an intolerable nuisance.'
[3] Ibid., App. A, part ii, 102a (in *Parliamentary Papers*, 1834, xxix).
[4] 5 & 6 Will. IV, c. 76, §§ 76–88, 92, 100, 112, 116.

IV

THE FREEDOM

THE charter of 1599 explicitly charged the corporation of Leicester with the good government of the artificers as well as of the other inhabitants of the borough.[1] Municipal regulation of economic life was a live issue in Leicester at least until the middle of the eighteenth century, and even after that the idea was not dead. Thus, although Adam Smith's strictures 'bore upon obsolete theory rather than current practice',[2] the ancient forms of economic regulation in the more conservative places showed a remarkable persistence.[3]

It is in the Leicester corporation's assertiveness in the economic sphere that we find the clearest evidence of continuity with the gild merchant. Until 1691 freemen's fines were entered in the chamberlain's account under the heading 'Chapman's Gild', a practice continued from 1380, when the parchment rolls ended and the lists on paper began.[4] Similarly, the corporation oath book, even when revised between 1763 and 1766,[5] retained in the chamberlain's oath the old phrases about improving the merchant gild, and the lands and tenements of the borough,[6] though this latter may imply nothing more than a merely legal continuity.[7]

There were also in Leicester a number of subordinate companies or occupations, of a type encouraged by the early Stuart government. The position of these companies in the eighteenth century is obscure, for lack of evidence. The proving of their ordinals and the appointing of their

---

[1] *Records*, III. 361.

[2] See Dowdell, op. cit., chaps. v and vi.

[3] Cf. MCR. 2016, 2021, for incorporated companies at Shrewsbury; 254, the glovers' company at Hereford. Cf. also the interesting treatment of this subject in E. Heckscher, *Mercantilism* (E.T. 1935), i. 237 ff.

[4] *Records*, II. xliii, cf. III. 101.   [5] MS. Oath Book.

[6] During the recordership of Robert Bakewell, whose handwriting occurs on the front page.

[7] For instance, in the mayor's oath in the same manuscript, those portions of it referring to the prohibition of forestalling and regrating are noted ' omit this ', which seems to point to the growing abandonment of the old economic morals.

stewards and wardens took place annually.[1] They were apparently used as a means of granting a partial freedom to trade in the borough, commonly for market days only,[2] and useful to outsiders.[3] Until 1756, freemen were still being sworn upon the ordinals of the various companies, butchers, cordwainers, carpenters, and the like.[4] How far these companies survived after the collapse of the corporation's authority in economic matters in the middle of the century it is impossible to say. There are no allusions to these bodies in the corporation records after 1756, and the municipal commissioners' report completely ignores them. Yet as late as 1800 the offence of selling bread under weight was considered gravely aggravated when the culprit was the steward of the bakers' company.[5]

With so restricted a sphere these 'under corporations' were not powerful in Leicester. Thus there were not in the town such disputes between corporation and under corporations as disturbed Northampton[6] and Norwich:[7] nor such assertiveness as there was at Shrewsbury, where the policy of the under corporations was held to have seriously hindered the town's prosperity:[8] nor were the Leicester occupations the recipients of charitable bequests as were the more independent organizations of Coventry.[9] Thus the municipal corporation, composed of men of

---

[1] Hartopp, *Register*, i. 535; *Records*, III. 300; Billson, *Mediaeval Leicester*, 123–39. For the difficulties of the tailors' company see *Records*, IV. xlii–xliii, 236, 238.

[2] As appears by CA. entries occurring till CA. 1729–30. Cf. also the interesting petition in *Records*, IV. 516, which suggests that the companies gave a partial freedom until a tradesman might be desirable as a 'settled person within the borough'.

[3] Cf. *Records*, IV. 373, undated petition of glovers of Mountsorrel.

[4] Hartopp, op. cit. From CA. it would appear that the most numerous holders of the partial freedom were butchers.

[5] *Leicester Journal*, 8 Aug. 1800. The passage referred to illustrates the decline of the regulations even in the companies, since it refers to the 'continuous depredations' of the culprit.

[6] Cf. Markham and Cox, *Records of the Borough of Northampton*, ii (1898), 276–7, 285.

[7] E. Lipson, *Economic History*, ii (1931), 48.

[8] MCR. 2021.

[9] *Account of the Many and Great Loans, Benefactions and Charities belonging to the City of Coventry* (1773), 9, 12, 17, 21, 22. Cf. *ELG.* iii. 425–6. For the decay of these companies at Bristol, *ELG.* iii. 450, n. 1.

trading, manufacturing, and agricultural interests,[1] was the only body that in the eighteenth century made any serious claim, effective or not, to regulate the town's economic life.

The basis of the corporation's authority in the economic sphere was the freedom of the borough. According to the charter of 1599, 'no merchant or any man who is not a freeman of the borough may use any trade or buy or sell other than in gross, except only in fair time, unless he has obtained the licence of the mayor, bailiffs and burgesses'.[2] The freedom was thus primarily an economic privilege, though it became by the nineteenth century largely eleemosynary and political. It was obtained, like the freedom of the old gild,[3] by the usual qualifications—birth, servitude, or purchase.[4] It had already been established that no woman could obtain the freedom.[5] Between 1689 and 1835 it became increasingly common for the corporation to grant the freedom for political or honorary purposes.

The most interesting features are presented by the qualifications of servitude and purchase. Even securing adequate civic control over the binding and making free of apprentices was not easy. In 1722, experience having shown the necessity,[6] the hall emphasized that, when apprentices for any reason had to change from one master to another, they should be 'turned over' before the mayor,[7] this a common regulation in municipal bodies. It was also necessary for the corporation to defend its control over the local apprentices against outside interference, as when in 1715 the London company of framework knitters, in its effort to establish control over the rapidly growing country industry,[8] threatened action against two masters

---

[1] It thus provides evidence if more were needed against Unwin's idea of the part played by under corporations in the conflict of trading and industrial capital; cf. Kramer, *English Craft Gilds* (New York, 1927).

[2] *Records*, III. 363. [3] Ibid. I. xxvii.

[4] MCR. 1896; Hartopp, *Register*, I. xv–xix. Persons qualifying as sons of freemen paid merely a small fine: the eldest free-born son, 'a pottle of wine'; the second son, five shillings; and third and other sons, ten shillings. There were of course perquisites to the town officials; see MCR. 1896.

[5] *Records*, IV. 596. [6] HB. 6 Feb. 1720/1, 19 Mar. 1722.

[7] HB. 12 Nov. 1722. Cf. *Records*, III. 136, 177.

[8] See W. Felkin, *History of the Machine-Wrought Hosiery* (1867), 72–9;

who had bound and made free their apprentices before the mayor of Leicester and not before the officers of the company.[1]

Soon after the revolution the Leicester corporation became divided in matters of policy about apprenticeship. The origin of these difficulties we may find in the diversity of custom in the country, this in turn due largely to the modifying of the principles of the statute of 1563, as a result of local custom and judicial interpretation. Interpretation was in fact a large part of the law. Disputes had led to judicial resolutions on the two questions: what trades were covered by the act, and whether it applied to villages.[2] The minimizing effect of the rulings of the courts weakened all corporations in their attempts to enforce a more rigorous practice, but neither of these two questions disturbed the corporation of Leicester. For, as to the first, the Leicester charter subjected all artificers in the borough to the corporation's rule, and the records supply no suggestion that there was any distinction of trades. As to the second, there are many instances of outlying freemen, living in villages, maintaining their privilege to take apprentices who should become free of the borough, by the customary payment of scot and lot.[3]

Most dispute arose in Leicester over the length of the servitude. This again varied from trade to trade. On this subject there was apparently in the corporation a division between 'laxists' and 'rigorists'. In 1696–7 the then mayor, John Roberts, bound three apprentices in such a way that their indentures were dated from 1693 and 1694. For this misdemeanour Roberts was ordered by the common hall to forfeit the salary enjoyed by the mayor for

J. D. Chambers, article 'The Worshipful Company of Framework Knitters', in *Economica*, 1927, 306 ff., and *Nottinghamshire in the Eighteenth Century* (1932), chap. v; F. A. Wells, *The British Hosiery Trade* (1935), 41–5.

[1] HB. 10 Oct. 1715.

[2] See R. Burn, *Justice of the Peace*, article 'Apprentices', for this topic; also J. Chitty, *A Practical Treatise of the Law relative to Apprentices and Journeymen and to Exercising Trades* (1812); for modern expositions see O. J. Dunlop, *English Apprenticeship and Child Labour* (1912), W. S. Holdsworth, *History of English Law*, xi (1938), 419–20.

[3] CA., e.g. 1715–16; cf. Gross, *Gild Merchant* (1890), i. 56–60; *Records*, IV. 430.

administering the apprenticeship law, a sum of £13 6s. 8d., paid out of the rent of the Gosling close. Twenty-three members of the hall voted for the punishment, four against.[1] Shortly after, an attempt was made to tighten up discipline by an order that the apprenticeship books should be regularly scrutinized before the mayor was paid.[2]

For some time the views of the common hall were unsettled, and the question came up again in 1718. For a short time the rigorists triumphed. In September the hall ruled that any person coming to bind an apprentice should swear that the apprentice was to serve as an 'Actuall Meniall Servant for the term of seven years to the trade or occupation mentioned in the Indenture of Apprenticeship before such Apprentice shall be bound'.[3] Such rulings were not unknown elsewhere.[4] It looks as if the corporation was trying to insist not merely on the seven years' servitude but seven years at one trade, in spite of the devices of lawyers to permit a certain movement from trade to trade.[5] It was probably directed also against the custom of an outdoor apprenticeship, though this did not become as common in framework knitting, the staple industry of the district, as it did in some other trades and places.[6] This order of September 1718, rigorous to a degree, was very soon 'destroyed and made void'.[7]

Apart from this short-lived severity, the corporation in general tempered justice with mercy, making concessions or refusing them, as seemed justified by individual circumstances.[8] Subject to this qualification, it sought in general to maintain the principle of a seven years' service. In this, it was no doubt strongly influenced by the woolcombers

---

[1] HB. 18 Mar. 1697/8 ; HP. xxii.

[2] HB. 5 July 1698.

[3] HB. 26 Sept. 1718.

[4] Cf. Lipson, op. cit. iii. 291.

[5] Cf. Burn, op. cit.; see also, for Dr. T. K. Derry's dissertation on the Statute of Artificers (Apprentices), *Abstracts of Dissertations . . . for D.Phil. Oxon.* iv (1931), 14 ff.

[6] See F. A. Wells, *British Hosiery Trade* (1935), 82.

[7] HB. 13 Oct. 1718.

[8] HB. 25 Aug. 1710, HP. xxi, instances of relaxation by which the custom of the borough was assimilated to general legal practice; in the case of Robert Fogg, the hall vacillated, refusing the freedom, HB. 21 Jan. 1718/19, granting it, Fogg having served only five years, 22 June 1719.

and clothfinishers, among whom the full period was greatly valued.[1]

It is difficult to know how far exactly apprenticeship in the eighteenth century had a genuine educational value, as its Elisabethan and early Stuart[2] promoters intended. The Leicester corporation appear to have valued it, and there were numerous charities in the town for apprenticing poor children, chief being that of 1760–2 of Gabriel Newton, who had himself been bred to the comber's trade.[3] Yet there are a good many signs that the institution was exploited for base motives. Thus in 1786 the archdeacon of Leicester, Dr. Burnaby, recommended the parochial visitation of poor apprentices, as a defence against their being ill treated, as they not uncommonly were,[4] and condemned the tendency of overseers for motives of economy to apprentice children to any master, regardless of the children's welfare, without taking care that the masters were good Christians.[5] Moreover, unscrupulous masters, where possible, tried to run whole establishments solely on the cheap labour of apprentice children, and against this practice of 'colting' the framework knitters in the first decade of the nineteenth century protested, even to the extent of ruining a master, Nicholas Payne of Burbage, who was a notorious offender.[6] Thus, though formal respect was still commonly paid to the admirable social objects of apprenticeship, and more than formal respect by some, in practice it often became a means of exploiting the weak, especially in village industry.[7]

Finally, in spite of the respect for apprenticeship shown by conservative benefactors, it was quite definitely on the decline, even in a district like Leicestershire, where numerous workers valued it. A statistical analysis of the register of apprentices shows that, though the actual number

[1] Lipson, op. cit. ii. 38, 75.   [2] Cf. *Records*, IV. 188.
[3] See below, p. 96.
[4] A. Burnaby, *Charge of 1797*, mentions a revolting instance of cruelty at Market Bosworth; *Leicester Journal*, 17 Mar., 15 Oct. 1797.
[5] Burnaby, *Charges of 1786 and 1787* (1788), 1, 14.
[6] *Leicester Journal*, 8 Apr. 1808; Felkin, op. cit. 435; J. L. and B. Hammond, *The Skilled Labourer* (ed. 1933), 227.
[7] Not only in the villages, of course; *Leicester Journal*, 13 Oct. 1797, reported a very bad instance in the town.

of apprentices bound even slightly increased, reaching its
peak between 1801 and 1810,[1] there was no increase in any
way comparable to the increase of population. Further, it
was in the chief callings that the decline was most noticeable.
Early in the eighteenth century, woolcombers and framework knitters had numerous apprentices, yet by 1829 the
former were enrolling none, the latter very few.[2] This
decline quite obviously reduced the importance of the
corporation in local economic life.

The freedom as obtained by redemption or fine[3] illustrates still further the decline of the corporation as a body
with economic functions. Every endeavour was made to
compel traders not otherwise qualified to take up their
freedom 'by purchase'. This was granted after formal
petition, by order of hall, on payment of a fine. This fine
steadily increased. In 1607 it was only £10;[4] in 1623
it was £20.[5] In 1735 an attempt was made to increase it to
£35,[6] but this order was never enforced on account of the
opposition it aroused.[7] In 1805 £30 became the actual
charge.[8] In 1824–5 fines of £50 were actually imposed.[9] In
1831 the corporation again reduced the fine to £35,[10] and
at this figure it remained so long as the old corporate system
continued.[11]

The purchased freedom had from the corporation's point
of view two merits : that through it corporate control over
the trade of the town could be extended, and the corporation coffers replenished. It had also advantages from the

---

[1] Cf. T. K. Derry, *Outlines of English Economic History* (1932), 166.

[2] These statements are based on the lists published in Hartopp, *Register*. It
is interesting to observe that Matthew Boulton, in the neighbouring town of
Birmingham, had no use for old-fashioned premium apprenticeship and developed
his own system of technical education ; see H. W. Dickinson, *Matthew Boulton*
(1936), 58–63.

[3] I have used the common expression 'by purchase', although it is not
technically correct : 'A corporation cannot make a bylaw that any person shall
be admitted by their officers to the freedom on paying a certain sum of money ;
for that were a sale of the franchise : but there may be a custom to admit
persons to the freedom, on payment of a certain sum of money, called a right by
redemption' ; J. W. Willcock, *Municipal Law* (1827), § 471, p. 187.

[4] *Records*, IV. 65.   [5] Ibid. 201 ; cf. 469.
[6] HB. 2 July 1736.   [7] Thompson, 77.
[8] HB. 21 July 1805.   [9] HB. 3 Sept. 1824, 14 Mar. 1825.
[10] HB. 5 Sept. 1831.   [11] MCR. 1895.

freemen's point of view, in that it conferred the right to trade in the borough, was a necessary qualification for any part in civic life, and opened the way to considerable charitable benefits. Against these benefits had to be balanced liability to civic service. It was probably on account of burdensome duties that, in spite of the benefits, there had been, at least since the middle of the seventeenth century, difficulty in persuading all the non-free tradesmen to take their freedoms.[1] In 1705 the plan was even tried of offering the numerous non-free woolcombers of the town their freedoms at the bargain price of £10,[2] but this produced no response. Within twelve months it was abandoned as 'prejudicial to the corporation'.[3] Possibly the woolcombers who held aloof set less store by the municipal freedom because of the advantage they derived from the wool-combers' 'tramping society'.[4]

A different view of the borough freedom was taken by the woollen drapers, who regarded the monopoly of trade, enjoyed in form at least by the freemen, as a protection. In a petition of uncertain date, apparently of the early part of the century, and perhaps to be associated with the ill effects on the woollen trade of the European wars felt after 1710, the woollen drapers, using precisely similar arguments to those of distressed apothecaries in the previous century,[5] sought to prevent the admission of strangers of their calling to the freedom. Formerly, they argued, the corporation had defended the chief trades, 'insomuch as they would not suffer any petition for the freedom of strangers to be read, gaining thereby considerable sums with apprentices incouraging and promoting the welfare of the whole borough'. Where the corporation had admitted

---

[1] *Records*, IV. 348, 485.

[2] HP. xxiii, common hall, 30 Aug. 1705; the text of the document in Thompson, 20–1.

[3] HP. xxi, minute of 12 Apr. 1706.

[4] S. and B. Webb, *History of Trade Unionism* (1920), 36–7. In Leicester Museum, 32. 23; a certificate of the admission of William Padgett of Gadsby, Leicestershire, woolcomber, to the company of woolmen of the city of London; also ibid. 33. 23, certificate that Thomas Parsons of Sawtry, Huntingdon, was allowed to bind and fold wool in the county of Huntingdon, by the constable of the company of merchants of the staple of England.

[5] *Records*, IV. 520–1.

to the freedom by purchase, it had been 'but to some ordinary occupations, where there was not a sufficient supply to manage the same'. In their own case there was no shortage of labour, and 'any of us can in our calling serve what may be needful'.[1] There is unfortunately no evidence how the petition was received.

We may take the language of this petition as revealing two things: first, that the freemen had enjoyed sufficient protection through the system of corporate monopoly confirmed by Elisabeth's charter to make their privileges worth defending;[2] and, second, that there was a fear that the corporation was beginning to abandon the use of the purchased freedom as a means of 'planning' or of rationalizing the labour market. This fear was justified. For the corporation came to regard the purchased freedom less as an element in an organized economic society and more as a source of revenue to be exploited.

The corporation was often in need of money, and its annual account quite often showed a debit balance.[3] It is also remarkable that the orders of hall for increasing the cost of the freedom in 1735 and in 1824 preceded expensive contested elections. Further, when the corporation embarked on particularly expensive projects, it commonly increased its pressure on the non-free to take up their freedoms. Thus at the time when the income from freedoms reached its highest point, so far as can be judged from the extant accounts, namely in 1753–4,[4] the corporation was busy with the election of 1754,[5] and with reorganization in the south field, the purchasing of the tithe and glebe, and repairs to property.[6] The increased income from free-

---

[1] HP. xxiv. Cf. with this *ELG.* ii. 398, n. 3: 'it is not clear whether the Freeman's so-called monopoly of trade had not—at any rate in many Boroughs —consisted . . . of an exemption from a tax upon traders'.

[2] Cf. HP. xxi, the petition of John Flavill, framesmith, which states that he 'being no freeman of the borough is forced to his great damage to work out of the liberty of the same'.

[3] e.g. CA. 1693–4, debit of £132 5s. 4¾d.; CA. 1701–2, of £120 14s. 6d.

[4] CA. 1753–4, £325 received for freedoms, of which £100 for purchases of freedoms.

[5] In which the freemen had political value as having votes.

[6] CA. loc. cit.: a balance in hand actually paid over to next year's officers of £656 17s. 0½d. (CA. 1753–4) was reduced to £127 by 1755.

doms at this time did not prevent a depletion of the corporation's balance in hand. By the middle of the eighteenth century the freedom had come to be regarded largely as a source of income to save an ill-administered corporation from bankruptcy.

It it obvious therefore that the corporation of Leicester was succumbing to the prevalent decline of economic regulation. The growth of the framework knitting industry in the town and district,[1] and the consequent increase in the power of the hosiers, also told against the economic claims of the corporation in the borough. For in fact the hosiery masters had left London for the provinces precisely to evade regulations of the type that the corporation of Leicester sought to enforce. It would be hardly too much to say that as the hosiery industry waxes the freedom declines. The freedom declines, but freedom increases.

Thus in the early years of the century it was hosiers that were prominent in the resistance to the corporation's claims, as when in 1705 the common hall, noting how many of the hosiers and other tradesmen were not free, arranged for a meeting of the mayor and four other members of the corporation with the non-free.[2] In consequence, a number of the illegal tradesmen took up their freedoms.[3] On the other hand, in 1706 the woolcombers, as we have seen, made no response to the corporation's advances,[4] and in 1709 threats of prosecution left their prospective victims unmoved.[5] In 1724 the corporation made an attempt to extend the monopoly to market days and Saturdays as well as ordinary weekdays.[6] This issue was settled by 1733, as the result of a campaign against non-free traders in general, and in particular against three glovers, by name Wing, Basford, and Stubbs.[7] The corporation's claims were dis-

---

[1] See Carte's account in Bodl. MS. Willis 85, fo. 49; the industry in 1716 employed some 7,600 hands in the town. Throsby, *History*, 401–2, calculates that in 1792 the industry employed 6,000 in the town alone, and there were about 70 employing hosiers and some 3,000 frames. See also Felkin, op. cit., for fuller statistics.

[2] HB. 5 Jan. 1704/5.   [3] Hartopp, *Register*, i. 195 ff.; cf. xxi.
[4] See above, p. 55.

[5] HB. 16 Dec. 1709; except that a watchmaker, Stephens, was successfully prosecuted, HB. 25 Aug. 1710; CA. 1710–11; Hartopp, op. cit. i. 205.

[6] HB. 10 July 1724; again HB. 6 May 1726.   [7] HB. 11 Sept. 1730.

allowed as for Saturdays and market days, but confirmed for ordinary days.[1] There followed at once a considerable movement of non-free tradesmen to take their freedoms.[2] On balance, therefore, the corporation's position was strengthened.

Yet still there was resistance, in 1736[3] and in 1740.[4] Still, intimidation had some effect.[5] Early in 1741 the corporation, in the use of its strongest weapon, the threat of legal proceedings, entered on the final and decisive contest, with its most stubborn antagonist, George Green, 'otherwise Smith', a non-free watchmaker.[6] Green was evidently a complete rebel, for while he was fighting the corporation he resisted also the parish of S. Martin's, by refusing to serve as a parish officer.[7]

It was not until 1749 that the case was finally settled by the defeat of the corporation in the court of common pleas.[8] Even after this reverse the corporation considered further measures against Green on the ground that he had libellously attacked the mayor.[9] It would be of great interest to know how this rebellious watchmaker was able so long to continue the fight; how far, if at all, it was because his own individual resources, which one would hardly expect to be immense, were supplemented by assistance from powerful interests in the town, such as possibly the hosiers, who were concerned to obtain greater freedom of trade; but on this point there seems to be no evidence.

However this may be, the final decision against the corporation should not have been unexpected, and the corporation's litigious aggressiveness in refusing the offer that Green made at one point, of £30 for his freedom, was as foolish as it was probably vindictive. For, as

[1] Throsby, *History*, 152; Thompson, 52. The contest was expensive, HB. 12 Feb. 1732/3; CA. 1732-3; Hartopp, *Register*, i. 251, 252.

[2] CA. 1733-4; Hartopp, loc. cit.

[3] HB. 2 Oct. 1736; Throsby, loc. cit.; Thompson, 77.

[4] HB. 24 Mar. 1739/40.

[5] Cf. CA. 1740-7; Hartopp, op. cit. i. 273-4.

[6] HB. 28 Jan. 1740/1.

[7] Leicester Cathedral MS., S. Martin's vestry book no. 19, 24 Jan., 1 Feb. 1741/2, 18 Apr. 1742.

[8] Thompson, 78-9; CA. 1749-50; HB. 1 Dec. 1749.

[9] 13 July 1750, for 'publishing a Libel against Mr. Mayor'.

Green's counsel observed, for years two women who were not free of the borough, nor were widows or daughters of freemen, had been able to carry on a business as milliners without any interference from the corporation.[1] In spite of the previous legal decisions, which had gone largely in the corporation's favour, it was obvious that the freedom regulations were in fact being more and more evaded.

Indeed the whole point was that the corporation could not satisfy the requirement of the courts that any restraint of trade must be proved to have existed as a completely invariable and uninterrupted custom so far as the memory of man would go.[2] The corporation, in pointing to an order of 1588 that all strangers must from thenceforth take up their freedoms, was in fact indicating evidence that told quite as much against it as for it. Further, the by-laws themselves were contradictory. For a by-law of 1610–11 allowed the non-free to trade on market days and imposed a fine in respect of other days, whereas, incompatibly with that, a rule of 1681 extended prohibition to market days also.[3]

The defeat of the corporation in Green's case did not for some time make any perceptible difference to the numbers of freemen enrolled.[4] This alone tends to show that the corporation was fighting a battle already lost, irrespective of the outcome of litigation. But the defeat of the corporation in Green's case was none the less of some consequence in the long run. For it deprived the corporation of its most valuable weapon. The non-free could no longer be coerced by judicial process. Thus of sixteen tradesmen who were threatened by the corporation between 1754 and 1758 only three took up their freedoms, and this only in the burst of political activity in view of an election.[5]

[1] Bodl. MS. Eng. misc. e. 55, fo. 79.
[2] See Parker's views in the important case of *Mitchel* v. *Reynolds* (1711) reported by W. Peere Williams, *Reports of Cases in Chancery* (1740), 184, 187.
[3] See, for the opinion of counsel consulted by the corporation, Throsby, *History*, 152 and n. (*a*); Nichols, i. 447 and n. 4. The case is reported as bearing on venue in H. Barnes, *Notes of Cases in Points of Practice in the Court of Common Pleas* (1792), 492.   [4] See Hartopp, *Register*, i.
[5] HB. 18 Oct. 1754, 1 July 1757; *Register*, i. 326, 327, 332; the three men were James Wightman, James Hallam, Edward Gregory.

The bottom was in fact taken out of the old gild economy so far as this had been perpetuated by the municipal corporation. The proportion of freemen to the rest of the population could not be prevented from getting steadily smaller, until in 1835 it was only 1 in 10.[1] All that was left of the old freemen's monopoly was that the beer-sellers of the borough had still to take up their freedoms, a custom that had its strength in the necessity of going to the magistrates for a licence. It was upheld by the court of king's bench early in 1833,[2] but abolished two years later by the clause of the Municipal Reform Act which set aside all trading privileges in corporate towns.[3]

The freedom having ceased to be of any economic significance, municipal regulation of the town's artificers was plainly not possible. The freedom became therefore primarily of political utility as an electioneering weapon, and as a necessary preliminary to entering the close corporation.

[1] MCR., app. i. 120; also 1897.
[2] *Leicester Journal*, 8 Feb. and 7 June 1833; HB. 19 Aug. 1833. In this case, *The Corporation of Leicester* v. *Burgess*, the point at issue was whether the recent Beer Licensing Act, 11 Geo. IV & 1 Will. IV, c. 64, applied to all the inhabitants of the town in such a way as to override any special privilege of the freemen. For the bad effect of this Beer Act, in multiplying beer-shops so as to increase drunkenness, see Webb, *History of Liquor Licensing in England* (1903), 114, 116.
[3] 5 & 6 Will. IV, c. 76, § 14.

V

THE GENERAL ECONOMIC POLICY OF THE CORPORATION

BETWEEN 1689 and 1835 the economic aspect of the midlands was very considerably changed. Roads were improved, canals made, and railways were begun. Birmingham grew into a large industrial centre, mines and smelting-works increased in the Black Country, the face of the country-side was much modified by large-scale inclosures, and above all, as most important for the town of Leicester, the hosiery industry, which had been introduced into the east midlands towards the end of the seventeenth century, grew miraculously.

Arguing strictly on the basis of the corporation's gild ancestry and the wording of its charter, we might expect that its policy in the face of these changes would be to follow the medieval, Elisabethan, and early Stuart precedents of attempted regulation. Quite apart from other factors, the decline of the freedom indicated the impossibility of this. What happened was something quite different. For a large part of our period the corporation consisted of individuals whose interests were not markedly different from those of the other inhabitants of the town. Being composed for the most part, like many other municipal bodies, of small business men,[1] it was not out of touch with the economic needs of the town community at large. Once the monopoly of the freemen was broken, there was no reason why the common halls might not serve to focus the economic desires of the town as a whole. None the less, we should be unwise to assume that the older tradition of economic paternalism inherited from the gild was entirely passed away, especially in view of the prevalence in midland counties even in the later part of the eighteenth century of seventeenth-century tory ideals.[2] For when division occurs in the town on matters of economic policy, we shall find that the corporation, in

[1] For a note on the personnel of the corporation see Appendix, pp. 154–8.
[2] Cf. L. B. Namier, *England in the Age of the American Revolution* (1930), 230 and n., 231.

the traditional tory manner, tends to support the reactionary policy of regulation, and to defend the small man.

The identity of interest between the corporation and the other inhabitants of the town was most marked where efforts were made to increase the accessibility of the town to a wider market. It is also worth notice that all the corporation's measures, like those of the gild, were taken in an intensely local spirit. Thus they had chiefly the object of strengthening the town as the chief trading-centre for the surrounding country-side, and indeed of the whole county. The local importance of the eighteenth-century county town appears most remarkably perhaps in the safeguarding of the town's fairs and markets, institutions that were particularly important at a time when ' apart from London, there was not a single town which had permanent business connections with the whole country'.[1] A description of Leicester in 1743 notes that the town is celebrated ' for one of the greatest markets in England for corn, cattle, and meat, on Wednesdays, Fridays and Saturdays: and for its fairs on the eve of Palm Sunday, the 1st of May, Midsummer Day, Michaelmas Day, and the 8th of December '.[2]

The Leicester corporation jealously guarded its fairs and markets. Thus it laboured to prevent competition arising from those of the neighbouring towns. In 1601 it had desired the abolition of all rival markets within a distance of eight miles,[3] an aspiration gratified in fact, though not in legal form, by their decay.[4] In the same spirit of local self-seeking, in 1699 efforts were made, even to canvassing of the earl of Stamford, to prevent the establishment of an additional fair at Market Harborough.[5] From similar motives the corporation, on the other hand, was willing to

---

[1] P. Mantoux, *The Industrial Revolution in the Eighteenth Century* (E.T. 1928), 111-13.

[2] *Leicestershire and Rutland Notes and Queries*, i (1889-91), 30; cf. Owen, *New Book of Fairs* (1788), 38-9.

[3] *Records*, III. xl. 441.

[4] W. Burton, *Description of Leicestershire* (1622), 4-5. 'The memory of those liberties is perished and forgotten, upon what occasion discontinued I know not.'

[5] HB. 13 Jan. 1698/9; CA. 1699-1700.

extend the scope of the Leicester fairs. Thus in 1731 provision was made for the selling at the Michaelmas fair of cheese,[1] and this cheese fair rapidly became an institution of some importance.[2] Again, as late as 1793 a plan was approved for increasing the number of fairs and maintained in face of opposition from the inhabitants of the streets where the fairs were held, on the grounds of noise, unpleasantness, and inconvenience.[3]

Still more important to the corporation were the markets. Especially now that the Crown, incorporating the duchy of Lancaster, had ceased to demand tolls and stallage dues from the market of the once mediatized borough,[4] the markets brought to the corporation a considerable revenue from the farming of tolls and charges. To the town also the markets brought great advantages, for they made it the great trading centre for the country-side. As well, they offered opportunity, otherwise denied in the first half of the eighteenth century, for the non-free tradesmen to ply their wares otherwise than in gross. Thus both corporation and town had an interest in 'improving' the market. Considerable sums were laid out by the corporation from time to time in maintaining the amenities enjoyed by the stall-holders.[5] Money was spent even on improving the appearance of the market place, chiefly by the ambitious rebuilding of the Gainsborough, Exchange, or market hall.[6] Finally, the great importance of the markets was reflected in the existence from early times of two officers especially connected with them, stewards of fairs and markets, as well as by the appearance during our period of two well-paid clerks of the market.[7]

[1] HB. 4 Aug. 1731. A May cheese fair mentioned, HB. 23 Nov. 1759.

[2] HB. 5 Sept. 1748, cheese storage provided for in the rebuilding of the 'Gainsborough'.

[3] HB. 29 Nov. 1793, 25 July 1794; cf. 5 Aug. 1808.

[4] For the difficulties of the Leicester corporation in securing complete control of its market, see *Records*, III. xlii–xliv, and for the starting of a wool market, ibid. xlv.

[5] HB. 8 Apr. 1715 (commissioners), new paving and building a new row of shops, thus producing a considerably greater income from rents; CA. 1715–16, the rents from the market-place shops were nearly four times what they had been in 1706.   [6] HB. 21 Mar. 1747/8; CA. 1747–8.

[7] MCR. 1900; MS. council minutes, report of finance committee, 13 Jan. 1836.

Especially were the Leicester markets useful to the textile and agricultural interests. For Leicestershire was one of the counties most affected by the eighteenth-century inclosure movement.[1] By the end of the century its importance as a centre of cattle farming was greatly increased by the work of Bakewell and his disciples in stock-breeding for the end of producing greater supplies of meat.[2] With the popularity of the new Stilton cheese, the Leicestershire cheese industry grew.[3] Finally, as Defoe and Young inform us, from the sheep-farms of Leicestershire the clothiers of north and west countries[4] and of East Anglia[5] obtained raw material, in the long wool of Leicestershire sheep.[6] Thus inclosure for pasture farming alone, quite apart from the arable farming of the western part of the county,[7] called for greater scope in the market of the county town for the sale of cattle, meat, and cheese. Just as the new fair of 1731 had been for the sale of cheese, so the new market of 1763 was for the 'sale of fat and lean cattle'.[8] Similarly, it was in response to a petition from graziers that the market-place committee was in 1823 empowered to establish a weekday market to suit the petitioners' convenience.[9] In these developments the corporation was, moreover, doubly interested. Not merely was it as proprietor of the market concerned to increase the yield of the market dues by fostering the interests of the numerous moderately small farmers of the county,[10] but it was itself the owner of extensive farming-lands let on lease.

In a similar way, the corporation's inherited responsibility for the economic welfare of the town, and the interests

---

[1] W. H. R. Curtler, *The Enclosure and Redistribution of our Land* (1920), 173, 206; Ernle, *English Farming Past and Present* (1912), 72, 168; cf. J. H. Clapham, *Economic History of Modern Britain*, i (1926), 19–22.

[2] Curtler, *A Short History of British Agriculture* (1909), 214–17; W. Marshall, *Rural Economy of Midland Counties* (1796), i. 359–61; cf. D. Defoe, *A Plan of the English Commerce* (1928 reprint of 1728 edition), 119–20.

[3] Marshall, op. cit. 320, 'Mrs Paulet of Wimondham . . . the first maker of Stilton cheese, is still living'.

[4] D. Defoe, *The Complete English Tradesman* (1726), ii, part ii, 54, 55, 59.

[5] A. Young, *A Farmer's Tour of Eastern England* (1771), letter i, 74.

[6] Cf. D. Defoe, *A Tour through England and Wales*, ii (1725), letter iv, 134–5.

[7] Marshall, i. 8.   [8] HB. 10 Mar. 1763.

[9] HB. 19 Mar.; *Leicester Journal*, 28 Mar. 1823.

[10] Ernle, op. cit. 194; Marshall, i. 13–15.

of its members, coincided with the desires of most of the inhabitants of town and county, in the support of projects to improve local communications by land and by water. These improvements were made more necessary by the remarkable growth of the hosiery industry in the surrounding villages, by the pursuit of more specialized forms of agriculture in the county, and by the great need of cheaper food. In spite of all the improvements that had been made both in the production and transport of food, there were still in 1765 and 1790 food riots in the town.[1] Coal was needed for fuel and lime for agricultural purposes.[2]

There is a good deal of evidence that the roads about Leicester were in a state of decay from which the parochial officials could not rescue them.[3] The Leicester corporation started its policy of giving support to road improvements in 1726, when it promoted the petition for a turnpike act for the main London road, between Loughborough and Harborough,[4] and by lending for a year the sum of £150, borrowed by it for the purpose, to the commissioners.[5] It was officially as a body well represented in the trust.[6] Next, in 1752, the corporation paid the cost of the first plan and estimates for the Ashby road,[7] a project that was claimed as his idea by a coal master of Swannington, 'clearly discerning at that time', as he put it, 'its great utility to the public, as also its certain advantage to my coal works'.[8] The Leicester corporation supported the petition for the act in the house of commons;[9] it borrowed in order to advance money to the Ashby road trust,[10] as it

---

[1] Throsby, *History*, 172.

[2] See *HCJ.* xxx. 177. Marshall, op. cit. i. 27 n.: 'Barrow, situated on the banks of the Soar, nearly opposite to Mountsoarhill in Leicestershire, has long been celebrated for its lime.'

[3] Cf. ibid. 35. Many illustrations might be cited, space permitting.

[4] HB. 26 Jan. 1725/6; *HCJ.* xx. 567; Pratt, *History of Inland Transport and Communication in England* (1912), 66; P. Russell, *A Leicestershire Road* (1934).

[5] HB. 21 Feb. 1725/6; 3 Feb. 1726/7, repayment demanded of £150.

[6] Statute 12 Geo. I, c. 5; Leicester Museum, MS. 15 D. 34. 1, minutes of the trust.   [7] HB. 8 Jan. 1752; CA. 1751–2.

[8] G. Holland, *Letter to the Inhabitants of Leicestershire* (1760).

[9] *HCJ.* xxvi. 531, 536; statute 26 Geo. II, c. 46; the mayor, recorder, and alderman of the borough of Leicester were trustees among others.

[10] HB. 17 Jan. 1752.

had done for the Harborough road, and in 1754 it joined
in demanding a needed amendment to the Ashby road act,
which had been so badly drafted that wagons and carriages
drawn by less than four horses had managed to pass toll-
free.[1] At the same time, in 1754, it promoted turnpike
plans for roads from Leicester to Uppingham and Wans-
ford [2] and Narborough and Coventry,[3] as well as later in
the sixties to Melton and to Lutterworth [4] and to Welford.[5]
Thus, starting significantly enough with the roads to London
and to the colliery district near Ashby-de-la-Zouch, the
corporation took its part in the improvement of all the
roads leading into the town. It was officially represented
by the mayor and senior members on the trusts. So
doing, it furthered the interests of its members as private
individuals, and of other residents in town and county, as
well as made possible an increased revenue from its fairs
and markets.

There was considerably less unanimity in the county
about the canal movement, which dominated the latter half
of the century, but in this, as in the turnpike movement,
the corporation upheld the common interests of the business community of the town. For Leicester the great
problem was the improvement of the river Soar between
the Trent and Leicester. This involved in part a navigation of the old seventeenth-century type,[6] in part the making
of new cuts. Such a plan offered great advantage to the

---

[1] *HCJ*. xxvi. 903–4; statute 27 Geo. II, c. 42.

[2] HB. 11 Jan. 1754 (loan of £63); CA. 1753–4: statute 27 Geo. II, c. 30;
the mayor, recorder, and 12 senior aldermen of Leicester were among the
trustees; as also the dean and prebendaries of Peterborough.

[3] HB. 25 Feb. 1754 (loan of £100); *HCJ*. xxvi. 903; statute 27 Geo. II,
c. 42; the mayor, recorder, and aldermen of Leicester were among the trustees
for the portions of the road covered by the act to Narborough and Hinckley; as
were the mayor and aldermen of Coventry and Warwick for further portions of
the road.

[4] HB. 4 Jan. 1764; *HCJ*. xxix. 756–7; statute 4 Geo. III, c. 84; this
statute provided also for branch roads off the Melton road to neighbouring
villages. The mayor and aldermen were among the trustees.

[5] HB. 22 Feb. 1765; statute 5 Geo. III, c. 78; the mayor and aldermen
were trustees. See also HB. 27 July and 24 Aug. 1810, when the corporation
ordered the removal of a windmill on its property at Knighton that was
endangering the safety of users of the Welford road.

[6] Nichols, i, pp. clix–clx; W. T. Jackman, *History of Modern Transportation*,
i (1916), 181; T. S. Willan, *River Navigation in England 1600–1750* (1936), 26.

town of Leicester, where were now being used great quantities of coal, which might be drawn from the Leicestershire coal-mines as well as from those of Nottinghamshire and Derbyshire. Yet in spite of the greater cheapness of water-carriage, and its value as helping to save the still very unsatisfactory roads from being made quite impassable by heavy traffic, canal plans excited everywhere diverse resistance.[1] The Leicester plan was no exception.

The first attempt to secure a navigation of the Soar up to Leicester, made in 1736, was totally abortive, for its promoters failed even to get a committee.[2] After this failure, the river was dealt with piecemeal. The first part of the plan, for a navigable waterway between the Trent and Loughborough, received legislative sanction in 1766,[3] but as floods near Loughborough made the execution of the whole scheme impracticable, an amending act had to be passed ten years later.[4] Only after long delay did the 'Loughborough navigation', completed within two years of the amending act,[5] give to Loughborough such an 'air of mercantile business' as excited the envy of the Leicester business men.[6]

Consequently, in the plans for making a navigable waterway between Loughborough and Leicester, the Leicester corporation took a more active part. The first attempt to secure a navigation of the Soar between Loughborough and Leicester, which was made in 1786, provided also for a tributary canal from Thringstone bridge on the edge of the Leicestershire colliery district to a place near Loughborough, and for railways running from Thringstone to the coal-mines. From Barrow, the Soar was to be canalized.[7] This plan received the active support of the Leicester corporation.[8] It aroused a powerful opposition. In so far as, by means of the Thringstone canal and railways, it aimed at preventing the Nottinghamshire and Derbyshire

---

[1] Jackman, i. 396–404.   [2] HB. 3 Dec. 1736; *HCJ*. xxii. 785.
[3] Statute 6 Geo. III, c. 94. The commissioners to whom disputes between the proprietors and holders of property affected by the act were to be referred included the mayor, recorder, and six of the senior aldermen of Leicester.
[4] Statute 16 Geo. III, c. 65; *HCJ*. xxxv. 522.
[5] Nichols, i. clx.   [6] *Leicester Journal*, 2 Jan. 1779.
[7] *HCJ*. xli. 270.   [8] HB. 24 Apr. 1786.

coal-owners from gaining, by means of a navigable Soar, a too advantageous position in the Leicester market, it roused the hostility of the proprietors of the Loughborough navigation, who derived great profit from the transport of coal from the north.[1] Similarly, while the new plan promised well for the coal-mines and lime-pits of Sir George Beaumont and the earl of Stamford, it threatened those of the earl of Huntingdon.[2]

Three years later, in 1789, a further attempt was made. This omitted the Thringstone canal, but provided instead for a navigation of the Wreake to Melton Mowbray. This plan also failed.[3] The final attempt began in 1791. The project was again loyally supported by the corporation.[4] This time it was planned that there should be stone roads or railways between the Loughborough navigation and the Leicestershire coal-field.[5] In spite of opposition, the projectors got their act in May 1791.[6] To gain this success it had been necessary that the proprietors of the Loughborough navigation should be guaranteed compensation against any loss that they might suffer from the new plan.[7] Similarly, in order to safeguard the interest in the Leicester market of Leicestershire coal-owners, provision had to be made for waterways in the Charnwood forest, with stone roads or railways at each end, joining their collieries with the Loughborough navigation, near its southern end. By this means they would have, with the projected 'Leicester navigation', a continuous route, largely by water, to the town of Leicester. The Leicester coal-owners' part of the plan, the Charnwood forest canal, was short-lived. Within a year it burst its banks. Since it was never restored to use, the Nottinghamshire and Derbyshire coal-owners were given a virtual monopoly of the Leicester market, which they enjoyed until the opening of the Leicester and Swan-

---

[1] *HCJ*. xli. 607, 633, 823.

[2] British Museum, 1865, c. 5 (28); a contemporary map arising out of the controversy about the scheme; see also ibid., map of 1785, K. 6. 41. l.

[3] *HCJ*. xliv. 214, 233; HB. 23 Apr. 1789.

[4] HB. 8 Mar. 1791.   [5] *HCJ*. xlvi. 167.

[6] Ibid. 430; statute 31 Geo. III, c. 65; Nichols, i, pp. clxi–clxv.

[7] The act stipulated that if the tolls of the Loughborough navigation fell below £3,000 the new company was to make good that sum.

nington railway.[1] In 1793 also, another act sanctioned the canal to Melton Mowbray that had formed part of the plan of 1789.[2] The Melton canal was by another act extended to Oakham.[3]

The Leicester corporation does not seem to have exerted its influence so strongly in favour of the making of the Leicester and Northampton canal, for which the act was obtained in 1793,[4] although it gave twenty pounds to the necessary widening of the west bridge.[5] The beggarliness of this measure of support may perhaps be explained on two lines: first, that the corporation was at this time concentrating its efforts on the Ruding tithe suit; and secondly, that possibly it was feared in the town that the Union canal project would make it easier for West Riding manufacturers, who supported the act,[6] to compete with the Leicester woollen and worsted wares, and for northern farmers to compete with Leicestershire farming produce,[7] in the London market.

Preoccupation with legal matters may have had the bigger influence, since the corporation did not find it impossible to support other canal plans farther afield. Thus in 1777 it very vigorously promoted the plan for the Erewash canal[8]; in 1783 it supported the scheme for a navigation of the Trent down to Gainsborough;[9] in 1810 for joining the Soar navigation, part of the Union canal, to the Grand Junction canal;[10] and in 1811 an abortive attempt to join Oakham, Stamford, and Harborough.[11]

---

[1] Pratt, op. cit. 242-3; Throsby, *History*, 413-19; in consequence the Loughborough canal shares in 1824 reached 200 per cent. Cf. Gardiner, *Music and Friends*, i. 93, who says that Derbyshire coal was first introduced into the town in 1791 by this canal.

[2] Statute 31 Geo. III, c. 77; the commissioners included the usual representatives of the Leicester corporation.

[3] Statute 33 Geo. III, c. 103.   [4] Ibid., c. 98.

[5] HB. 9 Aug. 1793; necessary if there was to be a continuous route from the Loughborough and Leicester navigations to the Nen.

[6] *HCJ*. xlviii. 257.

[7] Cf. Defoe, *Tour*, loc. cit., for Leicestershire and Lincolnshire meat supplies to London.

[8] HB. 25 Feb. 1777; *HCJ*. xxxvi. 251; statute 17 Geo. III, c. 69; the commissioners included the usual members of the corporation.

[9] HB. 28 Feb. 1783; *HCJ*. xxxix. 302; statute 23 Geo. III, c. 48.

[10] HB. 9 Mar. 1810; *HCJ*. lxv. 55, 193; statute 50 Geo. III (local 'to be judicially noted'), cxxii.   [11] HB. 29 Jan. 1811; *HCJ*. lxvi. 196.

The Leicestershire canal plans had thus a part in making a route by water from the east midlands to London. Generally speaking, we may say that the attitude to them of the Leicester corporation reflected that of the business community of the town. Similarly, when the Leicester and Swannington railway, the oldest part of the old Midland system, was first planned, it may have been, not less than the corporation's growing indifference to economic matters, the coolness of the rich men of the town, who had invested in canals and therefore did not favour the competition of the new railways,[1] that accounted for the corporation's having, so far as appears from the available evidence, officially taken no great account of the scheme until it was actually embodied in 1830 in a bill before parliament.[2] This, we may notice, contrasts remarkably with its enthusiasm for canals and turnpikes.

Finally, as a last illustration of municipal unanimity with the economic desires of the townsmen, we may notice the corporation's defence of the town's privilege of freedom from tolls throughout the realm. The corporation claimed for its freemen this immunity on the ground of its charters.[3] In the first half of the eighteenth century there were numerous disputes with other towns arising out of the wrongful exaction of toll upon the goods of Leicester freemen,[4] but after 1745 only one is recorded in the minutes, namely, in 1773, with Lancaster.[5] Until well into the nineteenth century, however, copies of the charters relating to freedom from toll continued to be issued to freemen for passing toll free, at sixpence a copy.[6]

Yet it appears from the most interesting of the actions

[1] See J. H. Clapham, *An Economic History of Modern Britain*, i (1926), 396. On the other hand, the original proprietors named in the act, 11 Geo. IV and 1 Will. IV, § lviii (local and personal), included a number of members of the corporation, four in all. The railway was the counter-move of the Leicestershire coal interest to regain the Leicester coal market, lost with the break-down of the Charnwood forest canal. See Pratt, op. cit. 243.

[2] HB. 2 Apr. 1830, because the railway needed land owned by the body.

[3] *Records*, III. xlii–xliii; IV. 74, 142–4.

[4] HB. 9 Feb. 1712/13, 16 Apr. 1715/16; HP. xxii (Derby); HB. 18 May 1723, 7 Feb. 1738/9 (Nottingham); 20 Feb. 1740/1 (Lincoln); 28 Nov. 1735 (Huntingdon); 26 Nov. 1703 (Bedford).

[5] HB. 20 Dec. 1773.

[6] HB. 19 Aug. 1697 (price fixed), 29 July 1812.

fought by the corporation that the charters were not always the best ground to take. In 1743 two beasts belonging to Thomas Ayre, a prominent member of the corporation, were seized on his refusing to pay toll on passing the ancient bridge of Bedford. The Leicester recorder thought the charters weak ground in this instance, for they specified only wares and merchandise, and cattle were hardly either. Nor did they mention pontage.[1] A more satisfactory argument for Ayre would be that Leicester was a town on ancient demesne and part of the duchy of Lancaster.[2] On both those grounds immunity could be claimed, unless Bedford also was ancient demesne. In fact neither party had a clear case.[3] In the end Ayre gained a favourable decision. The Leicester freedom from toll was in this instance vindicated.[4] This decision may be taken as reflecting the policy pursued by the judges, so far as was legally possible, of favouring internal freedom of trade.[5]

So far then, the corporation in economic matters has been able to speak for the town as a whole. When we come to consider certain problems that faced the corporation directly as a result of the growth of the local hosiery industry we find no such consistency. The corporation is at one time in agreement with the hosiers, at another hesitant, and at yet another in open disagreement with at least the most important.

First we find the corporation supporting the efforts of the hosiers to maintain advantages enjoyed by their trade. To a considerable extent, the Leicestershire hosiers, dealing in the woollen and worsted branches of the industry,[6] benefited from the policy of trade alliance with Portugal, which was embodied in the Methuen treaty of 1703, by

---

[1] Special appeal was made to grants of John, *Records*, I. 36; see also ibid. 53, for Henry III's grant of freedom from prises; cf. ibid. II. 228–9, charter of Henry V, which did actually mention pontage.

[2] Cf. PRO. DL 13/53, constats for passing toll-free.

[3] Press 24 (4), papers in *Ayre v. Hornbuckle*.

[4] Nichols, i. 623.

[5] Lipson, *Economic History*, iii. 288–9, 291.

[6] When Defoe wished to clothe his typical country grocer's wife from Horsham, he gave her stockings 'from Tewkesbury if ordinary, from Leicester, if woven', *Complete English Tradesman* (1726), i. 403; cf. his comments on the size of the industry in his *Tour*, ii (1725), letter iv. 133–4.

which Portugal received a good proportion of British woollen exports.[1] Anything threatening this advantage was to be opposed. Thus Walpole's 'excise', intended at first for wines as well as tobacco, excited the commercial fears of the Leicester corporation as well as offered a good chance to express a tory animosity to the whig minister.[2] Again, in 1745, the mayor of Southampton informed the Leicester corporation that a proposal was afoot to levy an additional duty of 4d. a tun on all Portugal wines. The common hall instantly determined on vigorous action. If the 'King of Portugal should lay a duty on Woollen Manufacture, it will prove very detrimental to this Country, and especially to this town'.[3]

We do not, however, find that the interest of the Leicester corporation was, so far as can be judged, at times more than intermittent. Thus when the Leicester hosiers' most profitable overseas market, namely that in the American colonies, was closed by the American boycott of English goods, after the Stamp Act of 1765,[4] the Leicester corporation does not appear to have actively concerned itself in the agitation for repeal.[5] It further appears that as early as 1788 Leicester business men were ceasing to regard the corporation as the natural organ for the expression of their economic desires, and the plan was mooted of a chamber of commerce.[6] Nor had the corporation, so far as can be discovered, officially any such part as it had had in the earlier road and canal

---

[1] J. James, *History of the Worsted Manufacture* (1867), 184, 203.

[2] HB. 27 Dec. 1732, 16 Apr. 1733; cf. Porritt, *Unreformed House of Commons* (1903), i. 267; S. Dowell, *History of Taxation* (1888), ii. 101–4, iv. 127–9; W. Coxe, *Memoirs of Sir Robert Walpole*, i (1798), 372.

[3] HB. 25 Feb. 1744/5; a deputation to visit Wigley, one of the members for the borough, at his residence at Scraptoft.

[4] B.M. Add. MS. 33030, f. 140, notes of evidence given at a committee called by the first Rockingham ministry, by a Leicester hosier, Joseph Bunney (the note-taker has 'Bumy'). See also L. Stuart Sutherland, 'Edmund Burke and the first Rockingham Ministry', in *Eng. Hist. Rev.* xlvii. 61–4; L. B. Namier, *England in the Age of the American Revolution*, 295–6; James, op. cit. 186–7; Lipson, *Economic History*, iii. 298–9.

[5] There is no reference at all to the question in HB. See below, p. 103, for the vote against repeal of A. J. Keck, one of the town members.

[6] *Leicester Journal*, 16 Feb. 1788; the immediate consideration prompting this proposal was to prevent the new invention for spinning wool by machinery from 'transporting the manufactory wholly from hence'.

projects, in the attempt made by local business men in 1832 to obtain a local court for the settlement of small debts.[1]

New problems were introduced by mechanical developments in the local industry. The earliest frame, which had been applied to the making of hose in Leicester towards the end of the seventeenth century, had strengthened the domestic organization of the industry.[2] But the expense of the frames gave the hosiers a great advantage at the cost of the poorer knitters, who had to hire the frames on which to work. The application of the new textile inventions to the hosiery trade in the later part of the century thus awoke a strong fear, especially as there was no scarcity of labour in it. The framework knitting industry remained most conservative until the latter half of the nineteenth century.[3] Thus in 1773 a new frame, the invention of a Scot, though placed in the Exchange by order of the mayor for safety, was none the less fetched out and smashed by an angry mob.[4] Again, in 1787 two of the largest worsted manufacturers in Leicester, Coltman and Whetstone, adopted the invention of Brookhouse, which applied the principle of Arkwright's method of spinning wool to worsted, only to find their efforts defeated by popular resistance.[5] Owing to an ignorance of economic law, which in the opinion of William Gardiner 'pervaded a superior class' as well as the lower orders,[6] this machine was pursued to Harborough, where it had been taken for safety, and there broken up. A mob in Leicester attacked Whetstone's house and those of other dissenters known to be his friends, and not until two hours had passed did the mayor and special constables try to quell the disorder, the mayor receiving a fatal

---

[1] *HCJ*. lxxxvii. 462. It would be interesting to know how far these plans reflected at Leicester the rise of a class of large employers, to whom the small masters got into debt. This was the case at Stockport (see G. Unwin, &c., *Samuel Oldknow and the Arkwrights*, Manchester, 1924, 35–6) and, I think, probably also at Leicester. If this suggestion is sound, we have further evidence, in a negative way, of the corporation's tendency to make common cause with the small man.

[2] F. A. Wells, *The British Hosiery Trade* (1935), 55; Thompson, 254.

[3] Wells, op. cit., chap. viii; Clapham, op. cit. ii (1932), 32–3.

[4] Nichols, i. 450; Thompson, 146–7.

[5] Nichols, loc. cit.; Gardiner, i. 82–4; Felkin, 229.　　[6] Cf. Thompson, 147–8.

wound from a stone which hit his head while he was reading the riot act.[1] Taking the evidence as a whole, the
corporation appears to have been somewhat hesitant in its
defence of the machines. It is fairly certain that the
majority of the corporation shared the ignorance and fears
of the poor riotous knitters, and as well were influenced
by a dislike of the nonconformist hosiers whose wealth
was a threat to their own power. No doubt also the
hosiers who were members of the corporation were jealous
of the progress of their dissenting rivals, such as the Coltmans, rich in the dignified possession of a big house in
the Newarke.[2] There was also an element of sheer economic conservatism in the outlook of a corporation that only
a generation before had fruitlessly defended an ancient
freemen's monopoly. On the other hand, the corporation
was dragged in the opposite direction by its duty of safeguarding property.

Hostility to the great nonconformist hosiers appeared
still more plainly in the last industrial crisis with which
the corporation concerned itself. Then the old-fashioned
economic morality was openly in conflict with the new
assertive *laisser-faire*. Under pressure of starvation wages,
the framework knitters revived their trade society, which
had for some time been moribund. In 1779[3] and again in
1812[4] they tried without success to obtain from the legislature prohibition of ' colting ' and a regulation of the industry. Finally in 1817, distress being unbearable, they
struck. The interesting fact is that the corporation magistrates regarded the strike with favour, and dealt very
leniently with men brought before them as offenders
against the combination laws.[5] Almost certainly they were

---

[1] Thompson, 185-8.

[2] For the family in general see the article by Mrs. Skillington, in *Transactions
of the Leicestershire Archaeological Society*, xviii (1934–5), 3 ff.

[3] *Leicester Journal*, 3 Jan. 1778, and a further reorganization, ibid. 14 Jan.
1791; Felkin, 115-16; Thompson, 163-4, 170. For a comment on wages
see Mantoux, op. cit. 432.

[4] *Leicester Journal*, 28 Feb., 6 Mar. 1812; *Reports of Committees of the
House of Commons* (1812), 37, 47; John Coltman's views, 100–1.

[5] *Report on Artisans and Machinery*, Fourth Report (1824), evidence of Thomas
Rowlett, 266. Perhaps it is worth recalling that Francis Place manipulated the
evidence at this committee so as to throw discredit on the combination laws.

influenced by the great burden of pauperism among framework knitters, especially since the overseers had adopted
the practice of paying premiums to manufacturers for
employing their poor. Still worse, the parish officers had
even directly employed them themselves. This direct
industry, not being run for a profit, was thus plainly a
cut-price industry, which embarrassed the conscientious
employer. As the distinguished nonconformist divine
Robert Hall explained, it tended to pauperize those
still in regular employment.[1] When the overseers had
agreed to abandon this pernicious but perhaps pardon-
able expedient, the employing hosiers granted the
framework knitters the improved scale of wages that
they needed.[2] They soon, however, declined from the
standard set up, and distress was quickly as bad as ever
again.[3]

The corporation had opportunity again to show its
sympathy for the knitters in 1819. In that year the knitters again appealed to the legislature for a regulation of
their industry. Again they failed in the face of opposition
from great hosiers.[4] It is interesting to observe that two
of the hosiers who were members of the corporation gave
evidence that tended to support a regulation of the industry,[5] while the wealthy John Coltman, a leader of the
local opposition to the corporation, was decidedly against
the policy.[6] The failure of the knitters' appeal in 1819
had interesting consequences, which showed how far the
corporation was now divorced from the most go-ahead
industrialists in the town. In October 1819 a relief committee was formed to maintain those framework knitters
who were thrown out of work in the fight for a decent

[1] Robert Hall, *Works*, iii (1845), 239.
[2] *Leicester Journal*, 14 Feb., 27 June, 4 and 11 July 1817; see also *Reports of Committees of the House of Commons*, 1819 (v), report on framework knitters' petition, 39, evidence of William Jackson, on the scale granted.
[3] *Report* (1824), 265.
[4] *Leicester Journal*, 22 May 1818, 12 Feb., 16 Apr., 18 and 25 June 1819. *Reports of Committees*, 1819 (v), ibid. 3–47, masters and men favouring this policy.
[5] James Rawson and William Watts giving evidence to the committee: *Reports*, op. cit. 13–21.
[6] In 1812; *Reports*, 1812 (ii), on petitions of framework knitters, 100–1.

livelihood.[1] The objects of this friendly society were lucidly
set forth by the powerful pen of Robert Hall in his defence
of the fund against the attacks of Cobbett. It was, he
said, 'proposed simply by means of voluntary contributions to afford a subsistence, scanty it will probably be at
the best, to that portion of the labouring class who are
destitute of employment, that they may not be compelled
to offer their labour for next to nothing, and thus reduce
the general rate of wages to the scale of depression which
has already been productive of calamitous effects'.[2]

This combination had the most influential support.
'There were allied on one side all the parish officers,
many of the masters, and all the men.'[3] The duke of
Rutland, lord lieutenant of the county, offered support,[4]
and a benefit night was held for the society at the theatre
under his patronage.[5] Parishes subscribed to its funds,
their interest enforcing the promptings of a benevolent
morality.[6] It is not surprising, therefore, that the Leicester
corporation should have been among the subscribers to
the funds.[7] The great were encouraged in their benevolence towards the efforts of the poor, a benevolence
particularly unwonted in the age of the six acts, by the
impeccable behaviour of the society. It carefully disclaimed
all illegal ends[8] and had its articles of association approved
by eminent counsel.[9] By 1823 both the finances of the
society and the benevolence of the great were wearing
thin. Yet still the corporation justices strove to maintain
a not unfriendly attitude. Thus, when the society's committee was summoned in 1821 for breaking the law, the
magistrates let it off with a warning.[10] Again, when
conditions were becoming intolerable, the children asked
bread, but could not be given by the magistrates more

---

[1] *Leicester Journal*, 22 Oct. 1819.
[2] R. Hall, *Works*, iii. 255–97; the passage quoted, 244. The whole affair is
an interesting illustration of Mrs. D. M. George's argument in *Economic History
Review*, Apr. 1936, vi. 172–8.
[3] *Report* (1824), 263.   [4] *Leicester Journal*, 22 Oct. 1819.
[5] Ibid. 26 Nov. 1819.   [6] Ibid. 7 and 21 Jan. 1820.
[7] HB. 28 Mar. 1820, 50 guineas; 11 Apr. 1821, £100.
[8] *Leicester Journal*, 7 Jan. 1820.   [9] Ibid. 22 Oct. 1819.
[10] J. L. and B. Hammond, *The Skilled Labourer 1760–1822* (ed. 1933), 253;
for a general account of the society, 250–3.

than a warning to be careful. Finally, in 1825, when a
strike broke out, warrants were issued against the leaders
of the society, and Hall's society came to an end. 'The
magistrates', it was explained, 'do not wish to be captious
or tyrannical towards a body of men who have in general
peaceably conducted themselves. But they owe it to the
public to keep the law.'[1]

This conclusion has for the historian of the Leicester
corporation a double significance. It reflects in two ways
the atrophy that took place in the economic functions of
the corporation between 1689 and 1835. First we see how
a last resistance was made by those still influenced by old
ideas of economic morality. We see also that the corporation from having been an organ through which the business community of the town expressed its views and policy
has become at best only the organ of a section. The
opposition of great hosiers was, as we shall see, of the
greatest importance in the political decline of the body.

The unreformed corporation's place in the economic life
of the town and county was necessarily to some extent
determined also by its being an owner of considerable
properties, especially in land, both near the town and
farther afield in the county. Moreover, the common hall
for a large part of the century included amongst its members
more than one fairly substantial farmer.[2] Consequently
the corporation had interests in common with the farming
gentry of the county, which were not without bearing (as
we have seen) on the corporation's use of its markets and
its support of improved communications. By 1835 this
basis of common interest was greatly diminished.

The real property owned by the corporation of Leicester
had diverse origins. From the medieval gild the corporation inherited a number of houses in the town, and lands
bequeathed by public-spirited citizens.[3] From the booty
of the Reformation it obtained by the charter of 1589,
besides the town 'obit lands', lands and revenues formerly
belonging to the two collegiate churches of the Blessed

[1] *Leicester Journal*, 15 Apr. 1825: bodies of framework knitters had been
picketing.
[2] e.g. Ayre, Phipps, and Oliver, for whom see below, p. 82.
[3] Thompson, 230-2.

Virgin [1] and the property of two of the dissolved religious fraternities, namely the gilds of Corpus Christi and of S. Margaret. In the seventeenth and eighteenth centuries there were added lands bequeathed for pious and charitable purposes,[2] as well as lands purchased by the corporation.[3]

Like most other corporations, the corporation of Leicester spent a great part of its energies on the management of its property. Since the time of James I there had been a separate body of 'commissioners for letting and setting the town lands', made up of the forty-eight senior members of the corporation.[4] In fact one of the chief advantages to be derived from membership of the common hall was greater opportunity of getting good land on the most favourable terms.[5] The importance of lands in the municipal scheme of the eighteenth century far outweighs their diminished importance in the new corporations of the Benthamite era. It is significant of this that the first professional officer of the Leicester corporation to be appointed, after the legal officers, was a steward of estates, or 'land steward'. This office appears definitely to have taken shape between 1794 and 1796.[6] Its appearance must have brought great relief to the overworked chamberlains, with whom traditionally the management of the corporation estates had rested.

[1] The greater church, in the Newarke, has now disappeared, but was the ancestor of the modern Trinity hospital (see A. Hamilton Thompson, *History of the Hospital and New College of . . . S. Mary in the Newarke*, Leicester, 1937, 230), and the lesser church now survives as the parish church of S. Mary de castro.

[2] e.g. *Records*, IV. xxvii. 242, 247–8, the land in Leicester forest which supplied Charles I's gift for the poor; ibid. 212–13, Christopher Tamworth's gift of lands 'for the maintenance of the weekday prayers' in S. Martin's church, of which particulars are in HB. 21 Sept. 1699.

[3] e.g. at Burbage and Frolesworth, HB. 3 Aug. 1724 at £1,060, of which Burbage land was afterwards sold to Edward Hood for £600; HB. 6 Apr. 1732. Gabriel Newton lent £200 towards the original purchase, CA. 1727–8. Similarly, land was purchased in the Horsefair, the purchase price being arranged by Gabriel Newton at £30, HB. 28 Jan. 1740/1; other lands in the Horsefair, 11 June 1764.

[4] See above, p. 7.

[5] See below for illustrations of this, pp. 83, 86.

[6] A Mr. Hole exercising the functions of a steward, HB. 4 Apr., 22 May 1794, 15 July, 27 Nov. 1795. Appearance of Edward Parsons as steward, HB. 19 Sept. 1796; salary of £100 attached to the office, HB. 4 Aug. 1800; Edward Parsons succeeded by William Parsons his son, HB. 17 Feb. 1819.

The land steward's office was all the more important since a very great proportion of the corporation's income came from its estates. Between 1699 and 1833 the rents of the corporation multiplied sixfold.[1] Needless to say, this remarkable increase was not accomplished without the vigilance of the corporation to improve and defend its estate. Thus the income from tithe was only saved for the corporation by a long legal battle. In 1769 the corporation aroused the hostility of the occupiers of the lands in the south and west fields, from which the tithe was drawn, by increasing the amount of composition that it exacted in lieu of tithe.[2] The rebellious occupiers were led by Rogers Ruding, a substantial whig inhabiting Dannett's hall. The point at issue was the ownership of the small or vicarial tithes only, which before the dissolution had been paid to the college of S. Mary de castro; not of the great or rectorial tithes, which as the quondam property of the dissolved Leicester abbey were incontestably the right of the occupiers. The corporation produced not merely Elisabeth's charter as evidence of its having entered into the rights of the dissolved college, but illustrated actual enjoyment of these rights by leases of tithe to occupiers of tithable land, the leases dating from 1604, 1790, and 1713.[3] In 1794 a decree of the court of the

---

[1] HP. xxii, calculation of the town clerk in 1698–9, that the rents due to the corporation totalled £633. 3s. 9d.: MS. Council Minutes, report of finance committee, 16 Jan. 1836, found that the income of the corporation from lands, &c., was as follows:

	£	s.	d.
Rent of lands and mills	2,453	3	4
Rent of houses	142	3	0
Chief rents	66	12	4
Tithes	242	16	5
Old market tolls	626	6	8
New market tolls	181	19	1
TOTAL	£3,713	0	10

[2] Leicester Town Hall, Press 24, papers relating to S. Mary's, deposition of John Lewin (chamberlain 1767–8).

[3] Press 24, ibid. Some of the salient historical points relating to the church of S. Mary de castro that were unearthed in the researches carried out by Lowdham, the town solicitor, in the record office (then in the Tower), the augmentations office, and the Bodleian library, for the purposes of this litigation, were copied from the papers in the town hall by the late Mr. Kelly, whose notes are now in the Leicester city central library, Kelly MSS., no. 12.

exchequer gave the victory to the corporation.[1] Consequently Ruding and his tenants were liable for arrears of
tithe that had accumulated while the suit was being tried,
which the corporation steward assessed at £2,314, the
corporation accepting the round sum of £2,000 in full
settlement.[2] The annual value of Ruding's tithe was put
at £114. 6s.[3] Joseph Cradock, the other chief occupier of
tithable land, paid £300 in composition of the arrears.[4]
The corporation's victory in the tithe suit thus established
its possession of a considerable revenue. It is worth
noticing, as a final point, that the corporation, being confirmed as 'lay vicar' of S. Mary de castro, was still responsible for the upkeep of the chancel of the church,
though these expenses were by no means considerable
by comparison with the income.[5]

The greatest problem before the corporation was not,
however, the defence of its tithe but the management of
the south field, one of the three ancient open fields of the
town. This was the only field with which the burgesses
as a whole and the corporation were greatly concerned in
the eighteenth century. For the common rights in the
west field had been eliminated in 1627–8 at the inclosure
of Leicester forest,[6] and the east field, though open till
1764,[7] was by the eighteenth century considered the
concern of S. Margaret's parish.[8]

The south fields, including adjacent meadows, consisted
of some 600 or more acres,[9] chiefly made up of the Grange
farm, which had formerly been the property of the dissolved college of the Newarke,[10] and had been first leased [11]
and then, in the early seventeenth century, bought outright
by the corporation.[12] This large area of agricultural land
lying to the south side of the town was additionally important because, unlike the overgrown modern city, the
market town of the early eighteenth century was a semi-

---

[1] HB. 4 Dec. 1794.   [2] HB. 21 Jan. 1796.   [3] HB. 27 Jan. 1796.
[4] HB. 14 July 1796; leased to him at £16 per annum for 10 years.
[5] HB., many references.
[6] *Records*, IV. xxxviii. 244, 370; C. J. Billson, 'The Open Fields of Leicester',
in *Transactions of the Leicestershire Archaeological Society*, XIV. i (1925), 9.
[7] Ibid. 13–14.   [8] Ibid. 13.   [9] Ibid. 16, 28.   [10] Ibid. 22.
[11] *Records*, III. 221–2, 252–3, 276.   [12] Ibid., IV. xxxiv, 135–6, 157.

rural community. The built-up area contained not merely houses but gardens and orchards. Townsmen could take as much interest as the country farmers in the cattle that came in every week to the Leicester market. Inhabitants, still possessing their own beasts, still valued their ancient right of pasture during commoning seasons in the common fields.

For long these rights had seemed in danger from the rise of larger farms in the south field. With the abandonment of the old strip cultivation, the commoners' pasture rights were increasingly disregarded.[1] It is in this connexion that the oligarchical character of the corporation most obviously appears. While it might have regard to the interest of the small man in manufacture, since the great manufacturers came to be its fiercest opponents, it was in agricultural matters on the side of the landlords, being itself one of them. It was to its financial interest to support the greater farmers in the fields against the commoners.

In the early part of the eighteenth century the corporation was divided, to the point of bitter altercations, about the best policy for the south field belonging to the body. In 1708 by a narrow majority the hall decided to obtain a bill for inclosure,[2] but in the face of opposition the attempt came to nothing.[3] In 1711 there were formal protests in the meeting of commissioners against the plan of splitting the corporation's estate in the S. Mary's fields into six farms.[4] It was probably as a result of opposition that in 1730 the corporation would not ' be at any expense about enclosing the south fields '.[5] The most bitter contest of the century came as the result of a lease of 550 acres

[1] Ibid. xxxvi–xxxviii.

[2] HP. xxi. 8, 9, and 23 July 1708; CA. 1707–8.

[3] A minority of three; it was decided to lay down the fields to grass and not to tillage, HP. xxi ; Billson, 25.

[4] HB. 29 Mar. 1710/11 ; 25 votes for, 7 abstained, 4 against, and 2 formal protests at the commissioners' meeting. As the two protesters had voted for the inclosure plan of 1708, their objection may have been to the commissioners' decision to put up the six farms to the best bidder, and not keep them comfortably within the corporate circle. Leases, HB. 15 Apr. 1710/11, all the lessees being connected with the corporation.

[5] HB. 3 Aug. 1730.

of land in the fields and meadows to three members of the corporation for a rent of £252. 14s., the lessees, Oliver, Phipps, and Ayre, undertaking to inclose the land in three large farms at their own expense.[1] Although express provision was made that the fields were to be laid open, from 1 September for the usual period, for the freemen to 'turn in their stint of cattle, in case the corn and grain of the said fields is then in', this did not suffice to allay the freemen's fears.

Immediately after the opening of the first commoning season that followed the letting of the land to the three farmers there were signs of serious anger on the part of the freemen. They held indignation meetings,[2] threw down fences, and damaged property.[3] Their indignation was, to adopt Throsby's phrase, 'big with mischeivous consequences',[4] and had a large part in the ferocity, unusual even for Leicester, of the parliamentary election of 1754.[5] The corporation, burdened with great expense in consequence of the riots,[6] sought to strengthen its position by a legal opinion. In 'Mr Caldecott's opinion' the necessary support was found for corporation claims. This eminent barrister ruled that the corporation might draw up leases reserving the right to permit such freemen only, as were thought fit, to exercise rights of common.[7] In the making of new leases this opinion was acted upon,[8] but not in such a way as to evoke further outbursts. After 1755 the excitement about freemen's rights ceased,[9] and the rearrangement of the fields in 1777–8 [10] passed off apparently without serious disturbance, in spite of an abortive attempt at this time to obtain an inclosure act, such as

---

[1] HB. 2 Nov. 1752.

[2] *Leicester Journal*, 10 Nov., 27 and 29 Dec. 1753; it seems likely that, as so often before, the corporation's tenants in the south field entirely or largely disregarded the clauses in their leases safeguarding freemen's rights, especially by turning out more of their own cattle than they had a right to do, and that the corporation, of which in this case they were members, abetted them.

[3] HB. 19 Sept., 24 Oct., 2 Nov. 1753, 26 July 1754; CA. 1754-5.

[4] Throsby, *History*, 157 n. (a); Nichols, iv. 347.

[5] W. Gardiner, *Music and Friends*, i. 207.   [6] CA. 1754-5.

[7] HB. 2 Sept. 1754; Throsby, *History*, 158-9.

[8] HB. 2 Feb. 1757; cf. Billson, 27.

[9] Thompson, 89.

[10] HB., meetings of commissioners, 18 and 25 Feb. 1778.

would have liquidated common rights.[1] The absence of disturbance in the next rearrangement of the fields, in 1795, in seven farms, and a large number of small lots, is almost equally remarkable, in view of the oligarchic provision that 'gentlemen of the corporation should have a preference' in the disposing of the small lots, and Mr. Chambers, as 'the father of the corporation', should have first choice of the larger farms.[2] This acquiescence in the corporation's policy in the fields, in the last half of the century, may perhaps be explained partly by the division into a large number of small lots[3] and partly by the growth of industry in the town, which, as we shall see, was making the outlook of many of the inhabitants of a more modern urban type.

It is not easy to arrive at a judgement, on the basis of the evidence available, about the corporation's views of the agricultural problems that were in this period matters of discussion. Its support of inclosures does not appear to have been informed by such an enthusiasm for a scientific agriculture as inspired Bakewell at Dishley, and those of his disciples, whose activities made this district so congenial to the itinerant Arthur Young.[4] The technical clauses of the leases show that the corporation was enlightened in its support of the use of clover, though it shared the common prejudice against potatoes,[5] the growing of which, in spite of their proved usefulness, appears to have been sanctioned rarely, and then generally to cope with food scarcity.[6] Generally speaking, it seems safe to say that the corporation supported inclosures, both in the south field and for its lands at Earl Shilton,[7] simply because as landlord it profited by the higher rents of inclosed land. This

[1] HB. 12 and 15 Sept., 1 Dec. 1777, 19 Jan. 1778.

[2] HB. 15 July, 27 Nov. 1795, 29 Jan. 1796.

[3] HB. 29 Jan. 1796, the lots let well; there were 48 small lots.

[4] A. Young, *A Farmer's Tour through East England* (1771), i, letter ii, 110 ff.; *Political Arithmetic* (1774), 146-7.

[5] HB. 18 Feb. 1778; tenants are not to sow their plots with any potatoes, garden seeds, or plants, but the corporation supplied 12 lb. of white clover per acre, the tenants refunding the cost.

[6] HB. 1 Apr. 1796, tenants may plant potatoes for one year; HB. 31 Mar. 1800, tenants may plant potatoes, beans, &c. 'early this year', but must sow corn the year following; the year following the land so used was to lie fallow.

[7] HB. 9 Feb. 1770.

impression is borne out by its attitude to Sinclair's general inclosure bill of 1796.[1] It was decided to express no opinion either way on this bill, 'as the operation of it may possibly affect some of the great manufactures of this kingdom, and amongst them that of this town'.[2]

But the most conclusive evidence of this view of the corporation's attitude is to be found in the inclosure act that was finally obtained for the south field in 1804.[3] Immediately after the conclusion of the purchase of the land tax on the corporation estates,[4] and of the contracting with corporation tenants for their purchase of fee farm and chief rents,[5] two very considerable pieces of business, the corporation felt itself able in September 1803 to initiate plans for the inclosure act.[6] After amicable discussion with representatives of the freemen, who nominated a commissioner,[7] the corporation nominating the other, the bill was drawn up and without difficulty passed into law,[8] so that, early in 1804, '3 Acts for the Enclosure of the South Fields were deposited in the Charter House'.[9]

The next seven years was occupied with the working out, in accordance with the general inclosure act of 1801,[10] of the details of the award, which task was completed by September 1811.[11] It was out of these labours that the south field committee emerged to supersede the commissioners.[12] The award gave to the corporation 453 acres, the larger part of the field, now free of common rights.[13] To the freemen, in lieu of their common rights, were allotted 125 acres, which were administered by freemen's deputies, elected by parochial meetings of freemen.[14] Be-

[1] *HCJ.* li. 433, introduced 24 Feb. 1796; Public Bills 1796–7.
[2] HB. 1 Apr. 1796.
[3] 44 Geo. III (private and local, not printed), no. 16; Nichols, iv. 348–9.
[4] HB. 7 Mar. 1799; transaction completed, HB. 4 July 1803.
[5] HB. 16 Feb. 1800, 6 Jan. 1801, 4 July 1803.
[6] HB. 9 Sept. 1803.   [7] *Leicester Journal,* 7 Oct. 1803.
[8] *HCJ.* lix. 78, 81, 94, 123, 135, 169, 180, 256 (royal assent 3 May 1804); HB. 27 Jan. 1804.
[9] HB. 29 June 1804.   [10] 41 Geo. III, c. 109.
[11] HB. 20 Sept. 1811.   [12] See above, p. 18.
[13] A considerable part of this was in compensation for glebe lands, and for 'all tithes of corn or grain . . . arising out of the said fields'.
[14] HB. 2 June 1821; a difficulty arose at first when the freemen's deputies refused to admit certain 'political freemen' appointed by the corporation for

sides these two principal allotments, 4 acres went to the Trinity hospital and about 10 to various proprietors. The final boundaries were arrived at only after considerable haggling between the interested parties.[1] Of the rest, land to the value of £600 was sold to cover expenses, and provision was made to accommodate the town horse race, for the building of one public and two private carriage roads, and as well for the preservation for all time of the New or Queen's walk, which the corporation had first laid down in 1785.[2] It was generally held in the town that the award was equitable. There was general satisfaction with this inclosure.[3]

Although it was one of the most successful ventures of the old corporation, the inclosure of 1804 contributed greatly to the opprobrium with which the unreformed municipality was assailed by the reformers. This inclosure emphasized the municipal separation from the economic life of the town. For the corporation had now its own estate, free of any obligation to freemen, and it intended to use this estate for its own benefit. These lands, like the rest of the corporate property, were, in town clerk Burbidge's view, ' the absolute property of the governing body of the corporation '; what was done with it was nobody else's business.[4] The end sought by the corporation was in fact purely fiscal. As early as February 1811 the inclosure had doubled the rent of the land and contributed more than any other step to the increased wealth of the corporation.[5] Indeed, it was maintained by the critics of the corporation that not as much profit was made out of the estate as might have

election purposes to share the benefits of the freemen's allotment. S. Nicholas church parish chest contains a minute-book of the parochial ' vestry ' that met to elect deputies for managing the freemen's estate, the first meeting recorded in the book being Tuesday 8 April 1806.

[1] HB. 21 Feb. 1805; Billson, 29.   [2] HB. 29 Apr. 1785.

[3] Billson, 28–9; *Leicester Journal*, 20 June 1805; Nichols, iv. 349. The summary here given is based on the actual award, which is kept in the town hall muniment room at Leicester.

[4] *HLJ*. lxvii. 399–400; cf. MCR. 1894.

[5] HB. report on finance and expenditure, 26 Feb. 1811 ; ' the total rental of that property in the year 1804 in its unenclosed state was only £963. 18s. 3d., whereas the net rental of it last year was £1894. 17s. 9d., being very nearly double '. The redemption of land tax and the purchase of rents brought an increase of £220 or more.

been. Although the municipal commissioners were informed by the corporation that land had been sold since 1810 to the value of over £20,000,[1] they believed that, in fact, at least some 30 acres had been alienated by private treaty at absurdly low prices to members of the corporation.[2]

In the long run the inclosure of 1804 was of much greater importance for the development of the town than the members of the corporation appear at the time to have noticed. For it greatly facilitated the urban growth of Leicester by removing common rights, which would have obstructed the building of new streets in its southern parts. Thus the growth of Leicester was not, like that of Coventry, hindered ' in consequence of the land which surrounds it being subject to rights of pasture on the part of the freemen, which prevents it being built on '.[3] The need for new streets also put money in the coffers of the corporation. In fact the valuation of corporation land in the south field grew so high that tenants complained to the steward of the impossibly heavy burden of parochial taxation thereby entailed.[4]

Along several lines we are therefore brought to the same conclusion. By the nineteenth century the Leicester corporation had not the place it had had in the town's life a century before. The forms of municipal regulation had broken down. The various attempts to improve communications had found the corporation, though at first active in the public interest, later falling away into indifference. The difficulties of the hosiery trade had shown that the corporation could no longer in any sense represent the strongest elements in the business life of the town. The development of the town lands revealed it as simply in the end a corporate *rentier*, at the best capable only of a spasmodic concern for the good regimen of a community of which it could in no effective way be considered representative. Divorced from the economic life of the town, its functions had by 1800 become for the most part, like the freedom, eleemosynary and political.

---

[1] HB. 24 Mar. 1834.   [2] MCR. 1903–6.
[3] MCR. 1839; cf. Maule and Selwyn, op. cit. 432 : ' There was no house upon the South Fields nor any inhabitant resident there until the year 1804.'
[4] HB. 6 Feb. 1817.

VI

CORPORATION, CHURCH, AND STATE, 1689–1790

GOVERNMENTS in the seventeenth and eighteenth centuries had a lively sense of the political importance of municipal corporations in the influencing of parliamentary elections. Charles I, Cromwell, and the Restoration monarchs all gave thought to the 'regulating' of these possible centres of political independence. After the revolution, the whigs, in 1690, sought to make the corporations safe for their own interest, in a manner hardly less inimical to liberty than the efforts that had earlier been made against themselves.[1] Hanoverian oversight was maintained by methods less spectacular, but not less effective.

Thomas Oldfield, in his *History of Boroughs*, observed that Leicester was 'neither under the immediate influence of Aristocracy or Administration';[2] and Robinson, in making his celebrated calculations before the election of 1784, numbered Leicester among the independent boroughs.[3] This independence was due to the great size of the constituency, which could muster two thousand or more voters.[4] This great size was, in its turn, due to the important determination of the house of commons in 1705 that the Leicester franchise was, as Charles II had designed, not confined to the companies,[5] but extended to include all freemen not receiving alms and householders paying scot and lot.[6] This democratic ruling, however, did not destroy (though it limited) the influence of the oligarchical corporation, since it had been held by the courts from the seventeenth century that corporations might with perfect legality make anybody

---

[1] Cf. T. B. Macaulay, *History of England* (ed. C. H. Firth, 1914), iv. 1779–83.

[2] T. H. B. Oldfield, *Entire and Complete History of the Boroughs of Great Britain*, iii (1792), 201.

[3] *The Parliamentary Papers of John Robinson 1774–84*, edited W. T. Laprade (Camden Series, 1922), 74.

[4] L. B. Namier, *The Structure of Politics at the Accession of George III* (1929), 101 n. 2, 106 n., cf. 114.

[5] Cf. H.M.C. (1930), *Papers of R. R. Hastings Esq.*, ii. 184.

[6] T. Carew, *Historical Account of the Rights of Elections* (1755), 321.

free, irrespective of residence, even if only for the purpose of creating a vote for an election.[1]

The power of manufacturing voters was not the only asset that the corporation enjoyed in its electoral battles. It had also a wide patronage. Thus, in performing services undoubtedly of the greatest value to posterity, the corporation, in its capacity of 'public trustee' for philanthropic endowments, at the same time was carefully husbanding for itself the armaments of political combat. The loan money, the schools, the alms-houses could all be exploited, without qualms of conscience, in an age when patronage was the sinews of war.

The political interests of the corporation no doubt very largely explain its care of its charitable endowments. A number of illustrations might be given of this. First we may note the great battle with the corporation of Coventry about Sir Thomas White's loan money. In 1542 White, the founder of S. John's college, Oxford, left £1,400 to the Coventry corporation to establish a loan charity to aid respectable young freemen of Coventry, Leicester, Northampton, and Warwick to establish themselves in independent positions. In 1692 it appeared that the income of the lands bequeathed by White was multiplied in value, but that the Coventry corporation was alone benefiting by this great increase. In 1696 the Leicester corporation joined with the other discontented corporations to open proceedings in chancery with the object of gaining a share in the increased income.[2] By decisions of the house of lords in 1702, and decrees of chancery in 1712 and 1718, the complaining corporations were successful.[3] In all the stages of the contest with Coventry the Leicester corporation had taken its share. It had its reward in the increasing by ten times of its income from this charity. It was able to institute loans of £40 in 1738, in addition to those already existing of £20 and £50[4]; and in 1825 to secure a decree

---

[1] Willcock, *Municipal Law* (1827), p. 188, § 472.

[2] HB. 29 Jan. 1695/6, 18 Mar. 1697/8; Nichols, i. 438.

[3] H.M.C. (1910), *House of Lords MSS. (New Series)*, v. 161–3; *Account of Charities connected with Coventry* (1802), 130, 150–75; HB. 17 July, 12 Dec. 1711, 23 and 27 Jan. 1720/1.

[4] HB. 20 July 1738.

of chancery for granting loans of £60, £80, and £100.[1] These large loans made the charity a really valuable weapon of patronage. It was indeed complained that the money went to wealthy supporters of the corporation, and not according to the founder's intent, to poor men. 'Port and claret men', it was said, 'have driven bread and cheese men very completely out of the field.'[2] At the end of its career the old corporation had a balance in hand of £2,000, a curious state for a loan charity. This was explained —it is true by a hostile witness, but probably correctly for all that[3]—as being due to the political use of the charity. 'It was well known that for any person to apply for a loan unless he had espoused the cause of the corporation, was a hopeless task.'[4]

For a second illustration of the importance attached by the corporation to its patronage we may turn to the large alms-house in the Newarke, the Trinity hospital. As this had been restored by James I,[5] the mayor, four senior aldermen, and the two chamberlains governed the hospital, under the duchy of Lancaster, as master and assistants. This foundation supported a hundred poor, and was regarded with pride by the corporation, which had maintained it out of its own funds in the difficulties of the interregnum.[6] Various members of the corporation had enriched the charity by their gifts.[7] In 1768 dispute arose between the corporation and the chancellor of the duchy of Lancaster, Lord Strange, because, whereas the master and assistants formerly had nominated to places in the hospital, now the chancellor took that right to himself.[8] According to Throsby, the root of the dispute was political. It arose as part of the election of 1768, when 'those in the opposite interest to the corporation secured the favour of recommending objects to the hospital on every vacancy'.[9] Appeal by the corporation failed to obtain restoration of their old privilege, but a satisfactory working arrangement was

[1] HB. 9 Mar. 1825.   [2] *Leicester Journal*, 18 Mar. 1825.
[3] The town clerk's explanation was very weak, see *HLJ*. lxvii. 390–1.
[4] Searson, 41–2.   [5] *Records*, IV. xxxv.
[6] B.M. Add. MS. (Liverpool Papers) 38446, f. 46 : Nichols, i. 345.
[7] B.M. Add. MS. 38446, f. 47.   [8] Ibid.
[9] Throsby, *History*, 301, n. (a).

arrived at, which left corporation patronage practically unimpaired, in that the chancellor of the duchy nominated according to the advice of the mayor.[1]

Yet with all its resources the corporation was only one among a number of competitors for the suffrages of the Leicester freemen and inhabitants. The gentry of the county appear to have had considerable influence in the town, and it was not uncommon for the borough members to be clients or relatives of the local nobility. Lawrence Carter, defeated candidate at Leicester in 1702, was a client of the powerful earl of Rutland;[2] in 1768 the combined forces of the earl of Stamford and the duke of Rutland defeated outright the corporation interest in the borough election;[3] in 1784 the Rutland connexion, in support of Pitt, had its representative in one of the successful candidates of that year, John Macnamara, in whose support the duchess of Rutland canvassed at Leicester,[4] as the duchess of Devonshire did at Westminster for Fox. In December 1789 Lord Rawdon wrote that 'with 6,000 voters' the Leicester contest would be 'desperately serious. I have no doubt that I could carry it, but it would be at enormous expense.'[5] The influence of these gentry in the town is not altogether easy to explain. Their wealth no doubt counted for a good deal in a greedy electorate, where there was already opposition to the corporation. To a certain extent also, the great magnates of the county could serve the corporation by influence in parliament and other high places. Thus the earl of Stamford was petitioned by the corporation to use his influence on its behalf in several matters[6] in the early part of our period; the duke of Rutland was approached by one of his group of members for advice how to vote in 1785 on the Leicestershire canal

---

[1] B.M. Add. MS. 381309, f. 117, Lord Hawkesbury to John Macnamara, M.P. for Leicester, 22 Sept. 1786, promising to continue this practice.

[2] H.M.C. *Rutland Papers*, ii (1889), 171.

[3] See below, pp. 104-5.

[4] H.M.C. *Rutland Papers*, iii (1894), 84; interesting in that the earl of Stamford is protesting to the duke against the duchess's activity.

[5] H.M.C. (1909), *Various Collections*, vi, MSS. of Captain H. V. Knox, 208 (Lord Rawdon to William Knox, 29 Dec. 1789).

[6] For the prevention of the Derwent navigation and the proposed Harborough fair in 1699, HB. 13 Jan. 1698/9; HP. xxii; CA. 1699-1700.

project then before the legislature.[1] Conversely, the great lords could use their influence in the town to get expressions of opinion on disputed matters, conformable to their political objects. Thus Macnamara in 1785 expressed the view that he could produce from Leicester, if it were necessary, a declaration that the Irish proposals of the Pitt ministry had caused them not the least apprehension.[2] Indeed, members often preferred to defy their constituents rather than anger their patrons.[3] Finally, in addition to their wealth, and the services that they could perform for the locality, the influence of the landed magnates in the town probably was fortified by the prestige habitually attached to the aristocracy. For, since the town was for the greater part of our period a semi-rural community, its inhabitants no doubt for the most part looked up to the lords of the county much as did the village rustics.

Yet it would be rash to conclude that the corporation of the borough and the aristocracy of the county lived always in the amicable relations of patron and beneficiary. There was a strong spirit of independence, in consequence of which the 'county' and the corporation were always competitors, often enemies. Indeed, until the middle of the eighteenth century, so long as the Leicester corporation was suspect of jacobitism, the great lords of the county, especially the earls of Stamford and Rutland, were the agents of the government in exercising a measure of oversight.[4] The presents of fat bucks that passed from these lords to the corporation had thus some degree of political significance, and were not merely occasions for succulent repasts when all the county was assembled at the mayor's feast.[5]

It is not easy to produce evidence of jacobitism that would conclusively demonstrate the guilt of the corporation.

[1] H.M.C. *Rutland Papers*, iii. 248 ; Thomas Thoroton to the duke, 13 Oct. 1785.

[2] Ibid. 198 ; David Pulteney to the duke, 7 Apr. 1785.

[3] Ibid., 'Smith of Nottingham and others are resolved to vote against the instructions of their constituents.'

[4] This was not, of course, an original policy.

[5] Cf. H.M.C. *Portland Papers*, ii (1893), 181 ; discussion of the county election of 1701 at the mayor's feast.

There was certainly a good deal of 'high church and Ormonde' sentiment in the town, but it was of a sort that appeared in the bibulous drinking by drunkards of the Pretender's health or the injudicious remarks of garrulous clergymen.[1] Throsby quoted the view that the corporation forfeited all respect 'for their rank and intelligence by choosing members from among the lower orders, of the meanest characters and abilities, those not attached to the king'.[2]

So far as the corporation records go, they naturally give no more evidence of jacobitism than may very temerariously be argued from possibly ambiguous phrases in loyal addresses to sovereigns of doubtful hereditary right.[3] In maintaining a vigilant watch over the corporation the government was no doubt concerned with the influence there of the jacobite earl of Huntingdon,[4] whose family was by long tradition associated with the town. It no doubt had also in mind the difficulties with members elect of the corporation who refused to take the necessary oaths qualifying them for office.[5] Apparently these suspicions of disaffection were sufficiently serious for the government to have them in view when quartering a large number of troops in the town; for the earl of Stamford, in urging on the town's behalf the reduction of this burden, attributed the long continuance of so large a detachment in Leicester to 'the ill-will of some persons who are afraid of the town growing honest'.[6]

The government's attention was especially drawn to the presence of disaffection in the town by jacobite disturbances there in 1722, 1738, and 1744. 1715, it will be noticed, passed without remarkable incidents. On the first of these

---

[1] SR. 1690, 1697, 1713.

[2] Cf. Gardiner, i. 202, 206. Gardiner is citing Throsby, *History*, 148, n. (*a*). Throsby is quoting from a letter accidentally made known, and is careful to point out that he does not approve of these strictures. 'I can discover but little more in it', he says, 'than a wish to obtain those places of trust which others enjoyed.' Gardiner does not quote Throsby's own view.

[3] Cf. Thompson, 91, 93.

[4] H.M.C. (1930), *Hastings Papers*, II. xiii–xviii.

[5] Thompson, 5; HB. 9 July and 29 Nov. 1691.

[6] *Cal. S.P. Dom.* 1694–5, 253; CA. 1692–3, payment for letters to the earls of Stamford and Rutland on this subject. Cf. Thompson, 45.

occasions of disturbance, in 1722, in the small hours of a July morning a company of seven or eight persons, whether after prolonged entertainment is not clear, proclaimed James III at the market cross of Leicester. The affair was brought before Carteret, secretary of state for the southern department.[1] The incident was an opportunity for the whig gentry of the county, led by the duke of Rutland, to demand that, as the town magistrates had, so it was stated, deliberately refused to take any action in this matter, the county justices should exercise a concurrent jurisdiction in the town. This demand was referred to the attorney-general for opinion.[2] The corporation was, however, protected by its charter. No doubt, a loyal address, conspicuously free from 'jacobite reservations', promptly sent off[3] convinced the government that the Leicester corporation could not be very dangerous.

In 1738 and in 1744 events took a not dissimilar course. In 1738 disturbance was caused by the publication in the town, in a singularly audacious manner, of treasonable papers reviling the Hanoverian succession. Judging by all the stir that was caused, these papers might have been the mainspring of a momentous conspiracy, whereas in fact they were trivial in the extreme. They were apparently part of the aftermath of a hotly fought local election. They were disclaimed by both parties. Probably rightly, they were regarded by one writer as a practical joke.

> While Leicester's sons, by party madness swayed,
> Forget their virtue, manners, sense, and trade,
> The wily scribler lies concealed from day,
> Surveys the tumult, and enjoys the fray.[4]

None the less, the government was alarmed, and letters passed between the mayor and the duke of Newcastle,

[1] HB. 19 Sept. 1722. No doubt the government regarded this Leicester episode more seriously on account of more ambitious jacobite plans at the same time such as the projected attack on the Bank of England.

[2] PRO. SP. 44/123, ff. 113, 229-30, 341.

[3] HB. 13 Aug. 1722.

[4] *Gentleman's Magazine*, viii (1738), 368, 557. The writer was probably William Bickerstaffe, a local clergyman who had a reputation for wit, for whom see Nichols, i. 320; *Gentleman's Magazine*, lix (1789), i. 182; Billson, *Leicester Memoirs*, 135-6.

secretary of state.[1] As in 1722, an attempt was made to secure for the county magistrates a concurrent jurisdiction in the borough, though only for the purpose of investigating the contradictory affidavits made to the town and county justices in this particular affair.[2] In 1744 again 'treasonable papers' appeared, and again there were communications with the secretary of state.[3]

At the time of the '45 the town was in great confusion and alarm. Needless to say, the corporation's enemies found at that time evidence of its jacobite sympathies. The only local efforts, apart from the marquis of Granby's 'Leicester blues', to put up any resistance to the Pretender's army, should it approach the town, were made under the leadership of dissenters, who used their burying ground for drilling such forces as they might muster. For the rest, many prepared to feed the invading army, a no doubt wise precaution in view of the marauding habits of the hungry Scots. The corporation contented itself with watching developments, and sent out messengers to find out whether the Pretender was coming farther south than Derby. There was also a rumour that the corporation prepared an address of welcome to the Pretender, to be used on his arrival, but that on the failure of the rebellion this was burnt. This jacobitical address—if it ever existed— may have been only a measure of insurance by trepidant burghers anxious for their property.[4] Even after the Stuart cause was dead, the corporation was still open to accusations of jacobitism, as when in 1766 the most groundless charges were made against mayor Fisher.[5]

There does not seem to be adequate evidence to show that the Leicester corporation was, even on the whole, jacobite. Like other persons of authority or consequence, the members of the common hall subscribed to the association for the defence of the revolution, which was formed after the assassination plot of 1696.[6] Well they might, for there were strong considerations that should have made

[1] HB. 22 Mar. 1737/8 ; PRO. SP. 44/130, ff. 310-11.
[2] Ibid., f. 300.   [3] HB. 22 Feb. 1743/4.
[4] Gardiner, i. 207 ; Throsby, *History*, 152 ; HB. 28 Nov. 1745 ; CA. 1745-6.
[5] See above, pp. 37-8.
[6] HP. xii (17 Mar. 1695/6) ; Thompson, 7, 60.

the members of the Leicester corporation think twice before supporting the recall of the Stuarts. Especially Leicester business men were interested in the prosperity of the woollen trades, which were counting for more and more in the economic life of town and county. They could, therefore, no more than Sir Thomas Hamner, the leader of the Hanover tories under Anne, a squire of similar economic interests,[1] afford the imperilling of the realm's material welfare that, as Walpole so well saw, would follow inevitably from a Stuart *coup*.[2] Further, the revolution itself had been the work very largely of tories, fearful for the safety of the church of England. Indeed, we may say that while the material interests of the corporation kept it from being a supporter of the non-jurors, its regard for the Establishment prevented it from supporting a popish pretender backed by 'foreign arbitrary power'.

For the corporation, though not jacobite, was certainly high tory. Moreover, its toryism was not merely that of the 'country' as against the court, of the 'outs' as against the 'ins'. It was the dogmatic toryism of the 'church party' of the reign of Anne. The tories of this school accepted the revolution; but they hated the toleration, which in 1689 had been scantily granted to the more orthodox of the protestant dissenters.[3] In this hatred of nonconformity the corporation persisted till its dissolution in 1836. There was thus in the local conflicts for political mastery a strong element of *odium theologicum*.

The zeal of the corporation for the Establishment showed itself in a variety of ways, not least in the infrequency of occasional conformity. Particularly interesting is the attitude of the corporation towards a local skirmish, part of the Trinitarian controversy that from time to time agitated the church of England during the eighteenth century. In 1719–21, and again in 1729–31, a whig priest, John Jackson, first confrater and then master of Wigston's hospital, was the occasion of fierce dispute by his preaching the

---

[1] G. N. Clark, *The Later Stuarts* (1934), 233–4.
[2] *EHR.* xv (1900), Basil Williams, 'The Foreign Policy of Walpole', 268.
[3] Cf. N. Sykes, *Church and State in England in the Eighteenth Century* (1934), 32–3.

doctrines of the Arian school from the pulpit of S. Martin's church, whose vicar was a high church tory divine, the antiquary Samuel Carte, a man of the utmost theological orthodoxy.[1] In the controversy the corporation supported Carte, who was congratulated by a sympathetic friend on having 'so good a mayor'. It was even suggested that, if the bishop should be unwilling to proceed against Jackson, the corporation might.[2]

Again, as a further illustration, there was the munificent benefaction of Gabriel Newton, alderman and mayor of Leicester, for the apprenticeship and education of poor boys, both of Leicester and of certain other towns, either as named in his will or chosen afterwards by the corporation as his trustees. This benefaction had its root in the devotion of the high churchmen of the eighteenth century, and especially in their devotion to the Trinity. Newton provided that his schoolboys should attend divine service daily, and be trained in the proper singing of the offices. It was also laid down that no place should benefit from this benefaction unless the Athanasian creed was duly recited in its parish church according to the rubrics of the English liturgy. In its efforts to overcome legal obstacles to its enjoyment of Newton's bequests, obstacles arising out of the mortmain law, the corporation showed great perseverance. In its careful organization of the schools, once its possession of the trust estates was assured, its aim was closely to follow the founder's intentions, and especially in the enforcement of the religious test. Thus it not merely secured another valuable instrument of patronage, but manifested a genuine devotion to those ideals cherished by alderman Newton.[3]

It was entirely in accordance with the 'high and dry' type of churchmanship such as the majority of Leicester corporation appears to have favoured, that no less a person than an alderman, on seeing the evangelical vicar of S. Mary de castro, Thomas Robinson, enter the pulpit of

[1] For an account of the Jackson–Carte controversy see my paper in *Theology*, xxix (1934), 276–82.

[2] Bodl. Carte Papers 239, f. 474, Montagu Wood to S. Carte, 17 Oct. 1721.

[3] I have described the early growth of Alderman Newton's Foundation more fully in *Transactions of the Leicestershire Archaeological Society*, xix, part ii (1936–7).

S. Martin's somewhat unexpectedly, should pick up his prayer book and ostentatiously walk out of the church;[1] or that the corporation itself should rebuff the evangelical agitators for the emancipation of slaves.[2] High church views again were reflected when, only a short time before Keble's 'National Apostasy' sermon at Oxford, the Leicester corporation received with high approval the discourse of a local curate, who set forth high ideas of the church, and a condemnation of dissent, much on the lines of the celebrated Oxford utterance.[3]

There was thus in Leicester a general coincidence of political and sectarian division. Apart from an active group of church whigs in the town,[4] it is generally true to say that the parliamentary history of Leicester in the eighteenth century was dominated by the mutual hostility of tory churchmen and nonconformist whigs. The local opposition had support from the great whig gentry of the county, especially from the earls of Stamford, and from the greatest of all the local potentates, the dukes of Rutland. As the local hosiery industry grew in size, and most of its leaders were opposed to the corporation,[5] the corporation party thus found itself faced with a formidable alliance of industrial, nonconformist, and aristocratic influence. The whiggery of the great aristocratic families of the county, who, as we have seen, aspired to bring the borough under their sway,[6] no doubt explains in part why the Leicester corporation was so decidedly tory. As with the lesser gentry of the county,[7] so in the town, toryism was an expression of 'independence', both of the great families and of the powers of the administration with which

---

[1] E. T. Vaughan, *Some Account of the Rev. Thomas Robinson* (1816), 64.

[2] HB. 16 Mar. 1826; cf. Vaughan, op. cit. 114.

[3] R. Maunsell, *A Sermon preached in S. Martin's church, on June 24, 1832*, printed by order of the corporation, 20–1, 21 n. Cf. also Vaughan, *Caesar and God* (1826), 36–7, a sermon also published by order of the corporation.

[4] Such as John Jackson, and later members of the Arnold family.

[5] Cf. the similar case of Taunton, where in 1784 the manufacturers were all dissenters; *Parliamentary Papers of John Robinson, 1774–84*, 39.

[6] As during the jacobite scares; see above, pp. 92–4, and below, pp. 159–61.

[7] In the county one member usually represented the Rutland interest, the other the independent freeholders; Oldfield, *Representative History*, iv (1816), 123–8.

the great nobles were commonly associated. A spirit of
municipal independence thus fortified sentiments of devotion to the church, in giving a strong tory colouring to the
corporation's public attitude.

Generally, the electoral influence of the Leicester corporation was great enough for the borough members in
the commons to think twice before plainly defying its
expressed judgement. We may therefore with fair safety
take the votes of the borough members on critical issues
in the commons, so far as these can be ascertained,[1] as
usually reflecting the opinions of the municipal oligarchs.
For the first sixty years of the eighteenth century the
Leicester members were in general to be counted amongst
the 'country gentlemen'. They were definite tories, though
not commonly of the most extreme sort. It is true that
Thomas Babington, one of the Leicester members of the
convention that met at the beginning of February 1689,
was amongst the substantial minority that voted against
the recognition of William and Mary as king and queen;
but this need by no means be taken as signifying a dangerous veneration for James II.[2] Indeed, the Leicester
members were not prominent in the blackest of *Black Lists*
of tories who were shy of the Association of 1696, or
accused of undue intimacy with a French agent in
1701.[3]

Until the latter part of the century the local whig aristocracy does not indeed seem to have met with great success
in its efforts to control a part at least of the borough representation. Even members with whig reputations or support
had a tory complexion. Even Lawrence Carter, burgess
elected for the town in the parliaments of 1690, 1698,
1701, and 1722,[4] who in his unsuccessful candidature of
1702 had the support of the Rutland interest,[5] and who in

---

[1] The division lists of this period are, it is well known, often very unreliable.
[2] *A Letter to a Friend upon the Dissolution of the Late Parliament* (1690); *A
Collection of White and Black Lists* (1715), 4; K. Feiling, *History of the Tory Party
1660–1714* (1924), 497.
[3] Their names do not appear in *A List of Members of one Unanimous Club . . .
that met at the Vine Tavern in Long Acre* (1702), or in *A List of those Persons said
to have been influenced by M. Poussin the French Agent* (1701).
[4] *D.N.B.* ix. 203.   [5] See above, p. 90.

1727 became a baron of the exchequer,[1] was 'a friend of
high "Church and King" principles'.[2] Still more misleading was the reputation enjoyed by James Winstanley,
member for Leicester with Sir George Beaumont from
1702 to 1714, of being a whig.[3] On a number of critical
occasions Winstanley voted, with Beaumont, in the tory
interest. His difference from Beaumont seems to have been
that he was not so faithful a supporter of Bolingbroke. In
1702, with Beaumont, he voted against the lords' provisions
'for the further security of the protestant succession';[4] in
1704 he was amongst the tackers in the persistent campaign
against occasional conformists;[5] and in 1710 he was one
of the supporters of Dr. Sacheverell.[6] Even the fact that
he voted, like a number of other tories, against the commercial treaty of 1713 with the French[7] cannot cause him,
after such a record, to be called a whig. In fact, in 1705
dissenters lamented his success against Carter on the latter's
attempt to unseat him.[8]

The whig ascendancy inaugurated by the Hanoverian
succession put the tories of the Leicester corporation yet
more decidedly on the side of the 'country'. Leicester
members with fair consistency voted against the party of
administration. In 1716 Beaumont opposed the Septennial
Act,[9] and the repeal of the Occasional Conformity and
Schism Acts,[10] though his fellow, Thomas Noble, apparently

[1] Cobbett, *Parliamentary History*, viii. 8; HB. 3 Feb. 1726/7; Carter,
formerly solicitor-general to the prince of Wales, later George II.
[2] Thompson, 246. See also Throsby, *History*, 183-4, for a brief account of
Carter. He was recorder 1696-1729.
[3] Gardiner, *Music and Friends*, i. 207; in reference to the election of 1754,
Gardiner notes a whig complaint that no whig member had been returned since
1714, at the election of Winstanley. Thompson, 246, speaks also of Winstanley
as a whig.
[4] *Collection of White and Black Lists*, 11; *A Test offered to the Consideration
of the Electors* . . . (1702); *Some Necessary Considerations relating to all Future
Elections* . . . (1702) gives only Winstanley.
[5] *Collection of White and Black Lists*, 33; cf. 36.
[6] Ibid. 16; *Compleat List of the Lords . . . with . . . Commons* . . . (1710).
[7] *Collection, &c.*, 27; A. Boyer, *Political State of Great Britain*, vi (1713), 14.
[8] W. T. Morgan, *English Political Parties and Leaders in the Reign of Queen
Anne* (1920), 127, citing Carte MSS. 125, fo. 94.
[9] *Parliamentary History*, vii. 372; *A Guide to the Electors of Great Britain* . . .
(1722), 8; *History and Proceedings of the House of Commons* (Chandler, 1741),
iii, Appendix.   [10] *A Guide*, 15.

abstained. In 1717 both members voted against the **Peerage Bill**.[1] In 1722 Noble was replaced by Carter, who, resigning in 1727, was followed at one remove by George Wright, a determined tory and grandson of the late lord keeper Wright.[2] Wright shared the representation of Leicester with Beaumont till the latter's death in 1737,[3] and after that with Wigley, Beaumont's successor, until he himself died in 1765. For practically half a century the Leicester members were of an undoubtedly 'tory' character. They voted consistently against Walpole: in 1733 in the battle about the tobacco excise;[4] in 1734 on Bromley's triennial bill;[5] and in 1739 in condemnation of the hotly discussed convention with Spain.[6]

For the first half of the century therefore we may conclude that the corporation maintained its hold over the representation of the town. By the middle of the century it was, however, clear that the opposition to corporation ascendancy had become formidable, and the corporation was forced to compromise with the enemy. The disputes of 1705, 1737–8, and 1754 reflect the increasing strength of opposition. The dispute about the election returns of 1705 is for our purpose interesting because the arguments of the two parties turned upon the freemen that were enrolled for each side. Winstanley's claim was only finally vindicated by the commons' reversing the decision of their committee, the dissenters so meeting a last-lap defeat. It was ruled that any voter having two votes must not appear to cast one, go away, and then come back to cast the other.[7] The

---

[1] Chandler, loc. cit ; *A Guide*, 22.

[2] *Parliamentary History*, viii. 8. T. Boothby Skrymsher till the end of the existing parliament; 615.   [3] Ibid. ix. 622.

[4] Ibid. viii. 1313 ; Chandler, loc. cit., on the vote as to bringing in the bill, only Wright against ; *A True and Exact List of Lords, &c.* . . . (1741) gives no information of Leicester members except that Wright was *for* the excise. *The Most Important Transactions of the 6th Session of the First Parliament of* . . . *George II* (3rd ed., 1733) gives both Beaumont and Wright as voting against the excise, as seems in my judgement most likely.

[5] *Parliamentary History*, ix. 479–80. In view of the events of 1737–8 at Leicester I feel justified in regarding the opposition of neither of the Leicester members as due to connexion with a discontented 'whig' faction.

[6] Chandler, vi. 7 ; *The Public having been imposed upon etc.* . . . (1739); *A True and Exact List* . . . (1741), 12.

[7] T. Carew, *Historical Account of Rights of Elections* (1755), 321; Oldfield,

election of 1737 presents still more interesting features
and shows still more plainly the influence of the whig
aristocracy. In this year the whigs put forward as their
candidate Ruding of Westcotes hall, and he was defeated
at the poll by the corporation candidate, James Wigley.
His friends petitioned the commons against this return.
In 1738—while this petition was under discussion—the
treasonable papers were spread abroad in the town, their
object being in the opinion of leading tories to discredit
the corporation in the eyes of the commons, and so to
influence the final ruling on the petition. In the affair of
the papers we have already observed the activity of the
duke of Rutland, intriguing against the corporation.[1] The
defeated whig partisans complained that the excessive
number of outvoters had been the cause of their defeat,
and therefore made it their aim to obtain a restriction of
the town franchise to residents in the borough.[2] It is not
easy to see exactly what difference such a change would
have made, unless the calculation was that the constituency,
being reduced, would be more amenable to aristocratic
influence, and the corporation would be deprived of the
useful weapon of being able to grant non-resident freedoms
for purely political purposes.

The disputes of 1705 and 1738 were, however, mere
skirmishes in comparison with the battles of 1754 and
1768. In 1754 local whigs, backed by the whig gentry
of the county, saw a good opportunity in the discontent
widely felt among the freemen at the corporation's plans
for inclosure in the south field : and put up as their candidate a Major Mitford. In his support, the Rutland family,
setting up as defenders of the freemen's rights, were so
popular as never to appear 'but they had the acclamation
of the people'.[3] The whig mob, led by a Winstanley,

Representative History, iv (1816), 125; Nichols, i. 440; Bodl. MS. Willis 48,
fo. 364, MS. Carte 125, fo. 94; *HCJ*. xv. 135-7.

[1] See above, p. 94.

[2] *A Full and True Account, being an answer to the remarks of a lying Faction*,
London, 1738; this was a reply to the corporation party's *Faction Unmasked*,
with Remarks etc., Stamford, 1738. There is a copy of this latter in MS. Carte
114, ff. 469-70.

[3] Gardiner, *Music and Friends*, i. 41; Gardiner, who is not always accurate,
gives as supporters of what he calls the 'liberal cause', besides the Rutlands and

marched to the fields and pulled down the corporation's fences, in accordance with an advertisement they had issued beforehand.[1] Both sides were active in the enrolling of freemen, some eight hundred being enrolled on the eve of the election.[2] According to hostile testimony the corporation party imported into the town some 'three hundred colliers . . . from Coleorton Moor armed with bludgeons in which iron spikes had been inserted to support the tory cause'. These attacked the whig committee room so that portly whig gentlemen not unnaturally fled.[3] The corporation triumphed in this contest, and Wright and Wigley were satisfactorily returned. A petition against this return was unsuccessful.[4] It is important to notice that the corporation to a man voted for the successful candidates, and that, although the defeated whigs made the usual complaint that the outvoters had disproportionately influenced the result, the poll-book shows that the tory candidates had a majority, though not a large one, amongst the town voters.[5]

The election of 1754 is a very significant event in the political history of Leicester. So hardly fought, it clearly illustrates three points of some interest: first, that the opposition is now more aggressive, organized, and powerful; second, that purely local discontent is still of as great importance in local elections as national issues; and third, that the corporation's success depended in large part on its internal unity.

With the accession of George III to the English throne a new situation was created in English politics. It has been pointed out that the pseudo-toryism of George III's régime cut across the old tory ideas of local independence.[6] This

Stamfords, 'Sir John Danvers, Sir Woolstan Dixie, Sir Arthur Hazlerigg, the Packs, the Hartopps, Pochins, Kecks, Simpsons, Winstanleys &c.'
[1] *Leicester Journal*, 22 and 29 Dec. 1753.
[2] Hartopp, *Register*, I. xxxiv. 289–316.
[3] Gardiner, i. 207. [4] *HCJ*. xxvii. 37–8, 279.
[5] From the poll-book I calculate that of the outvoters the tory candidates had 430 as against 278 for the whigs; votes from the borough and liberties I calculate as being 780 for Wright and Wigley and 718 for Mitford. From the county I find 282 for Wright and Wigley, 13 for Mitford and one other candidate, and 149 for Mitford alone.
[6] L. B. Namier, *England in the Age of the American Revolution*, 210–11. It is tempting to conclude that we may see evidence of the changes brought about by George III, in George Wright's being numbered among the opponents of the

confusion does not appear immediately to have affected the Leicester corporation, for Wright and Wigley were without difficulty returned to parliament in 1761. This new situation may, however, account partly for the dissensions in the corporation between 1765 and 1768. Division was also, in all probability, caused by the controversies about the American stamp duties, which were imposed in 1765 and withdrawn in 1766. Although there was strong disapproval of the Stamp Act among the merchants of Leicester, the corporation apparently preferred the assertion of constitutional claims, at the expense of prosperity, and the new member for the town, Anthony James Keck,[1] voted against the repeal.[2]

The first signs of difficulty arose in consequence of the need to elect a new member on the death of George Wright in 1766. At first two candidates offered themselves, the recorder, Robert Bakewell, and Edward Palmer. Palmer withdrew on seeing the strength of Bakewell's support.[3] As he withdrew, an express message from London announced the candidature of John Darker, a London merchant owning lands in Leicestershire, who stood on the old platform of 'Church and King'.[4] The corporation became quickly split into antagonistic parties of 'Bakewellites' and 'Darkerians'.[5] Bakewell's election address appealed especially to the trading interests in the town,[6] and his party were interestingly enough dubbed as 'presbyterians'.[7] On the second day of the poll he retired, and Darker's London votes, 120 in number, were therefore stopped at Dunstable by express.[8] Darker was therefore elected, and, soon after, Bakewell severed all connexion with the corporation, being

administration on the subjects of general warrants and seizure of papers in 1763, and of the same party as Pitt, James Murray, and the Cavendishes; see *Parliamentary History*, xv. 1406, amongst 'the absent Members supposed to be in that interest'.

[1] Wigley having died in 1765; *Parliamentary History*, xv. 1082.
[2] Almon's *Parliamentary Debates 1765-8*, vii (1772), 144; *List of Minority in the House of Commons against Repeal of the Stamp Act* ('Paris', 1766), 5.
[3] *Leicester Journal*, 25 Jan. 1766.   [4] Ibid.
[5] MS. Berridge, 109'30/34, 8.
[6] *Leicester Journal*, 25 Jan. 1766.
[7] MS. Berridge, 109'30/34, 8 and 9.
[8] *Leicester Journal*, 1 Feb. 1766.

dismissed from the recordership for insulting the mayor and other aldermen in open session.[1]

Divisions in 1766 prepared the way for catastrophe in 1768, for the house divided against itself could not stand. There were two candidates on each side : Darker and Palmer for the corporation; and for the whigs Booth Grey, a near connexion of the earl of Stamford, and his friend Colonel Eyre Coote. Both sides prepared for a fierce battle, and numerous freemen were enrolled.[2] The poll lasted a fortnight, a fortnight of hectic alarm for peace-loving citizens. The outcome was a total defeat for the tories. Aided by the influence of Groby and Belvoir, Grey and Coote were returned as members for Leicester. It was now the tories' part to complain about outvoters, but with as little reason as usually attended that complaint.[3] The general election of the year was generally marked by great venality,[4] and the Leicester contest was not an exception. The contemporary annalist of Leicester, Throsby, was deeply moved by the spectacle of universal bribery. 'In vain', he sighed, 'did Cassivellaunus, Caracticus, Alfred, Harold, Montfort, the barons under King John, Russell, Sidney and their followers struggle and suffer for such a corrupted progeny.'[5]

The reason for the corporation's spectacular defeat may be sought chiefly in two directions. Primarily, it was due to internal faction. On the last day of the poll, seven aldermen and twenty-one of the common councilmen went in a body to vote for the whig candidates.[6] To a less extent also, it seems probable that the connexion of the Rutland interest with the successful repeal of the Stamp Act contributed to the popularity of candidates of its party in a mercantile community. The whigs, as commonly since

[1] HB. 11 Apr. 1766.   [2] Hartopp, *Register*, i. 352–61.
[3] Poll-Book, 1768; I calculate the votes as follows :

			votes in all	outvoters	borough votes
Grey,	votes in all,	1,366;		536;	830
Coote	,,	,,	1,334	,, 520	,, 814
Darker	,,	,,	1,284	,, 513	,, 771
Palmer	,,	,,	1,260	,, 507	,, 753

[4] Cf. Mahon, *History of England* (1841), v. 289.
[5] Throsby, *Memoirs*, v. 129–31.
[6] Poll-Book, 1768, 174–5. It is interesting that this company included Sismey and Pocklington, whose disfranchisement had been attempted in 1766.

1754, were able to play on old grievances in the inclosure
of the fields.

Above all, then, the election of 1768 showed how pre-
carious was the corporation ascendancy in face of so strong
an opposition. The corporation, to insure against a repeti-
tion of this defeat, began almost immediately to offer the
freedom to gentlemen 'of known constitutional principles',[1] this systematic activity being plainly directed to
evade the 'Durham Act' of 1763, which invalidated the
votes of freemen of less than a year's standing.[2] Within
little more than a year some 250 had been enrolled, being
for the most part clergy and gentry resident in the county.[3]
The church and lesser gentry were thus called in to
counteract the growing influence of the dissenters and
manufacturers. These measures strengthened the corporation, but not enough to regain for it its former ascendancy.
All that could be achieved was a compromise, similar to
that usual in the county, according to which one candidate
was returned for each of the contending parties. Thus in
1774, and again in 1780, Grey and Darker were returned,
one for the corporation, the other for its opponents.[4]

It has been common for these two members to be
regarded one as tory and the other as whig or 'liberal'.[5]
Yet when their parliamentary activity is examined, neither
appears as generally a supporter of the administration.
Especially, it is significant that all the four members from
Leicestershire, both town and county, supported Dunning's celebrated motion against the unduly great influence
of the crown.[6] The conclusion to be drawn seems fairly

---

[1] HB. 1 May 1768.   [2] Statute 3 Geo. III, c. 15.

[3] Hartopp, *Register*, i. 361–8.

[4] *Leicester Journal*, 8, 22, 29 Oct. 1774; a contest was threatened at Leicester
by Bakewell's putting up as a candidate, but averted by the withdrawal of 'that
ambitious disappointed man'; ibid. 16 Sept. 1780.

[5] Gardiner, i. 41, 207–8, uses the word 'liberal'.

[6] See the interesting *Correct List of Members of the House of Commons*, which
sets out the votes of members on 'certain public questions in which the rights
and liberties of the people were essentially concerned'; published by Almon,
1780. Grey voted against the administration on three of these questions: in
Apr. 1777 on a grant to pay the king's debts, without vouchers; in Apr. 1780
on Dunning's motion; in Apr. 1780 on the prorogation before petitions, &c.,
were complied with. On this last occasion Darker voted *with* the ministry. In
Feb. 1780 he voted against it on the list of pensions, &c.

obvious. The terms 'whig' and 'tory', apart from the church question, had in Leicester little positive content. The old country spirit of local independence was strong, after the accession of George III, both with the corporation and with its opponents. The issue therefore between the two is narrowed down. It is the purely local issue of the town's 'independence', interpreted differently by contending parties. A Leicester 'tory' sought municipal independence from aristocratic interference; a Leicester 'whig' sought to secure for the citizens, especially for the nonconformists, independence of the corporation's control, especially in the election of members of parliament.

Darker died in 1784, but his successor held his seat only a short time.[1] In the crucial general election of 1784 a fierce contest began at Leicester, so fierce that one candidate of each side withdrew, leaving the town to be represented by Charles Loraine Smith and John Macnamara, the latter standing in the Rutland interest.[2] Thus in form the compromise of rival parties, maintained since 1774, was continued—yet with a difference. For the corporation party and the Rutland interest agreed in opposition to the Fox–North coalition[3] and in support of the younger Pitt.[4] Both parties in Leicester were now 'ministerialists'.[5] The 1784 election marks a revolution in the political history of the Leicester corporation. After 1790 it becomes increasingly plain that the fight for 'independence', both from aristocratic influence and from oligarchical control, must be taken up by more revolutionary hands.

---

[1] *Parliamentary History*, xxi. 777; succeeded by Shuckburgh Ashby.

[2] *Leicester Journal*, 3 Apr. 1784; HB. 12 Apr. 1784; freedom of the borough offered to Macnamara; *Parliamentary History*, xxiv. 784.

[3] HB. 19 Jan. 1784; address to Crown against Fox's India proposals; cf. HB. 21 June 1725, corporation invests in East India stock.

[4] HB. 6 Feb. 1784: 'the freedom of this borough be presented to the Right Honourable William Pitt for his firm and manly support of the Constitution in this time of imminent Danger when daring and ambitious men would wrest from the best of Kings his just right to the appointment of his Ministers'.

[5] *Parliamentary History*, xxv. 475; it is interesting that both the town members were in the minority on Pitt's proposals for parliamentary reform, though in this they hardly represented general corporation opinion, see below, p. 109; HB. 1 Jan. 1789, resolution in support of Pitt's regency policy.

VII

THE CORPORATION AND RADICAL REFORMERS
1790–1830

THE concord of 1784 between the Rutland interest and the corporation party in support of the younger Pitt was strengthened by the startling events that, before the expiry of the parliament then elected, had entered upon their course across the Channel. The Parisian attempt to put into practice the Utopian theories of not unfashionable revolutionary intellectuals, and especially the attack by the peasants of France on their. seigneurs' *châteaux*, alarmed the conservative and the propertied in England, whatever their political connexions. Encouraged by Burke, whig gentlemen for the most part threw in their lot with their hereditary rivals, to defend their common interest in the *status quo*. Thus, we may say, the French revolution completed what George III had begun, the creation in England of what we may call a 'national government' interest under Pitt.[1] In consequence, the minority of the 'whig' opposition to George III that persisted after this in hostility to his administration were bound ultimately to move to the 'left', and to join forces with reformers of a more subversive type. By Lord John Russell's alliance in 1818 with the radicals,[2] this inevitable conclusion was reached.

This schism of old and new whigs had considerable bearing on the history of the Leicester corporation. For as Gardiner complains, with the French revolution the whig families and landowners of Leicestershire 'surrendered all their former notions of liberty, and joined the tories in supporting old governments and abuses'. The only persons not to share the general panic were in his view Lord Moira, Sir Francis Burdett, and Mr. Ruding.[3] Yet

[1] It has been pointed out that this was only the completion of tendencies already set in operation by the difficulties of the first decade of George III's reign. See K. G. Feiling, *The Second Tory Party 1714–1832* (1938), especially 127, 139, and chs. x and xi.

[2] G. S. Veitch, *The Genesis of Parliamentary Reform* (1913), 349.

[3] Gardiner, i. 209–10.

it is arguable that the conservative panic of the great whig families was in the long run a benefit to the political opposition in Leicester. The withdrawal of the greater part of its aristocratic support meant that it had now to stand on its own feet. It was now at liberty to grow out of the sterile whiggery of the propertied aristocrats, interested chiefly in their own electoral influence, into the more constructive radicalism of the Bentham school.[1]

Above all, the direction of the battle against the corporation now fell to the leaders of the local chapels. Most important of these was the Great Meeting, in 1790 still presbyterian, but before long to become unitarian.[2] Amongst the influential dissenters, men of respectability and substance,[3] we should specially notice a group of local manufacturers, notably Coltman, Brewin, and Whetstone, all spinners, and as well the bankers' family of Paget.[4] These men were supporters of almost anything that threatened tory privilege; or that embarrassed the Establishment. Bunyan, and later Wesley, preached in the same room at the Coltmans';[5] Priestley and Howard were entertained by the Brewins.[6]

The meeting-houses of Leicester thus became citadels of reform, while the parish churches became associated with resistance to all change, which could be traced to 'jacobinical' or 'levelling' principles. To adopt a modern terminology, long-standing sectarian differences became commonly connected with a newer contest of 'ideology' and Utopia. From the corporation's point of view, it was therefore greatly alarming that in Leicester, as in many other towns, 'Salems for every dissenting sect are springing up everywhere, but nobody builds new churches'.[7] The important class of intelligent artisan found in the meeting-house an escape from the sycophancy too commonly associ-

---

[1] Cf. Place's evidence, B.M. Add. MSS. 27809, fo. 40: 'The French Revolution produced a great change . . . it induced men to look beyond mere party squabbles . . . to think for themselves.'
[2] A. Herman Thomas, *History of the Great Meeting, Leicester* (1908), 26–7, 54, 60.
[3] HB. 16 Jan. 1822.
[4] Gardiner, i. 56, 62; Billson, *Leicester Memoirs*, 89, 15–26, 32–4.
[5] Gardiner, i. 311. [6] Idem, i. 63, 73.
[7] *Leicester Journal*, 22 May 1818.

ated with the parish church, and as well social organization
of a more democratic type.[1] Even the followers of the tory
John Wesley could not escape the levelling influences of
dissent.[2] Moreover, the influence of the great Dr. Priestley
was making the dissenters more politically conscious than
ever before. ' Religious Liberty ', he had informed his
readers in 1774, ' is indeed the immediate ground on which
we stand, but this cannot be maintained except upon a
basis of Civil Liberty.'[3]

The Leicester tories noted these developments with
alarm. In 1782 the common hall was horrified by even the
moderate suggestions of Wyvill's Yorkshire committee for
a parliamentary reform. Such efforts as those of the committee, to improve upon the ' unparalleled excellence ' of
the constitution, were branded as ' unnecessary and un-
proper . . . when we are braving the exertions of a World
in Arms '.[4] In 1790 worse was to follow, in the dissenters'
holding at Leicester a meeting of their deputies, under the
very noses of the aldermen and councilmen. In a series of
resolutions now almost famous, the common hall declared
that ' the admission of Dissenters into Civic Offices would
give them perpetual opportunities of injuring the State by
applying the Powers with which they would be entrusted
to the support of their own Party '.[5] Opposition to the
local oligarchy thus almost inevitably made a man a dissenter. Even more than the eminently respectable Revolution Club, which had been founded under the patronage
of the whig aristocrats after the election of 1768,[6] the
radical societies of the war and post-war period, such as
the Friends of Peace in 1812,[7] the Hampden Club formed

---

[1] This is not, of course, to ignore the social distinctions inside the ranks of
dissent.

[2] Cf. E. R. Taylor, Methodism and Politics 1791–1831 (1934), and R. F.
Wearmouth, Methodism and Working Class Movements 1800–50 (1937).

[3] J. Priestley, Address to Protestant Dissenters (1774), 1.

[4] HB. 17 Jan. 1783, against a proposal of parliamentary reform in the commons in this year; Wyvill Papers, ii. 108–10; but cf. p. 106, n. 5.

[5] HB. 23 Feb. 1790.

[6] Gardiner, i. 41.

[7] Leicester Journal, 27 Nov. 1812; led by two radicals, Coltman and Ryley,
together with two nonconformist divines, Mitchell and Berry; it was in Berry's
pastorate that the Great Meeting became unitarian.

in Leicester in 1816,[1] and the supporters of Queen Charlotte in 1820,[2] were predominantly nonconformist. Even an attempt to form a Constitutional Society in 1821 to ' oppose the present alarming progress of disloyal and seditious principles ', by uniting on a common platform whigs and tories, churchmen and dissenters,[3] could not take away from the local opposition its virile nonconformist leadership.

Reforming politics in Leicester were, moreover, associated with worse even than the socinianism of rich worsted-spinners. The local opposition was influenced by a small group of intellectuals, free-thinkers, men regarded by their contemporaries as positive infidels. These had as their centre the Adelphi Club, a philosophical group founded by that remarkable Leicester bookseller Richard Phillips.[4] This society met originally to study natural phenomena, but soon turned to the study of political writings, of a subversive type, such as Mackintosh's *Vindiciae Gallicae* and the writings of Paine.[5] The corporation allowed itself to get alarmed at the thought of a few intellectuals reading ' left ' literature, and welcomed the proclamation of 1792 against seditious publications.[6] In 1793, acting under instruction from the government, the local justices paid a shoemaker to buy from Phillips's shop certain of Paine's works such as made mock of the most venerable English institutions. Phillips was found guilty of selling seditious literature, on the count of Paine's *Rights of Man part the second*, other counts being left,[7] and he was sentenced to eighteen months' imprisonment. It seems fairly plain, especially as other

---

[1] PRO. HO 43 (Hampden Clubs, i), Burbidge to Sidmouth, 18 Oct. 1816, seeking emergency powers for the justices to deal with this menace. For the alleged connexions of Leicestershire Hampden clubs with Luddism, see Wearmouth, op. cit. 33, and F. O. Darvall, *Popular Disturbances and Public Order in Regency England* (1934), 136, 161, which latter rightly discounts the evidence of spies on this point.

[2] *Leicester Journal*, 29 Sept., 24 Nov. 1820.   [3] Ibid., 12 Jan. 1821.

[4] See *D.N.B.* xlv. 210–11, article on Phillips; he became sheriff of London and was knighted.

[5] Gardiner, i. 73–4.   [6] HB. 7 June 1792.

[7] SR. 1793; on the count of the *Jockey Club*, a special verdict left points to be decided on a future verdict; as to Paine's *Letter to the Addressers* (on the subject of the proclamation of 1792), he was acquitted, this being not quite certainly ' seditious '.

booksellers who had sold the offending work went scot-free, that Phillips was victimized, as the leader of the young radicals of the town. Above all, he was the owner of a radical propagandist newspaper, the *Leicester Herald*, which was 'maintained on principles of civil and religious liberty'.[1]

Phillips left in jail another member of his club, George Harley Vaughan, a master at the grammar school. Aristocratic connexions did not save Vaughan from a sentence of three months' imprisonment for distributing seditious literature in the form of a pamphlet denouncing the war with France.[2] In consequence of his conviction, Vaughan lost his post at the school,[3] which the corporation evidently feared was being tainted with 'left' opinions.[4] Shortly after his release, Vaughan committed suicide, to be afterwards regarded as 'indeed the martyr of Leicester liberalism'.[5] Another radical, George Bown, was also charged with sedition about the same time, but not successfully.[6]

These persecutions do not appear to have prevented the spread of dissenting opinions in politics and religion, but rather served in the long run to increase the unpopularity of the oligarchy. Especially the tories failed to establish their influence over the respectable artisans of the town. This is particularly evident from the history of the Leicester Mechanics' Institute. This was started, in 1826, under the patronage of aristocrats and churchmen, but soon fell under the control of the 'levelling' or 'deistic' party. By 1835 it was regarded as an apanage of the liberal party, because it was 'chiefly supported by Mechanics, who vote in opposition to the Corporation at the election of the two Members of Parliament'.[7] Significantly also, from the lowest class

---

[1] Gardiner, i. 74–6; *Leicester Herald*, 6 and 20 Apr. 1793.

[2] SR. 1794; *Leicester Herald*, 3 May 1794; Gardiner, i. 76. Vaughan was convicted merely by reading a handbill he had been given, and passing it to one other person.

[3] HB. 2 Sept. 1794.

[4] HB. 6 Jan., 24 Feb. 1797; new rules provide for the removal of the master if he holds 'any Principles which may be subversive of Religion or the established Government of the Country'.

[5] Thompson, 212.

[6] *Leicester Herald*, 24 and 31 May, 2 Aug. 1794.

[7] G. Holt, *A Complete Exposure of . . . the Mechanics' Institute* (1835), letter 2nd, p. 5.

of worker, the Institute drew no support, but only from the more intelligent and respectable.[1]

It is evident, therefore, that the liberal opposition of the early nineteenth century found its strength where formerly the corporation had obtained the basis of power, namely in the developing industrial life of the town. Since the corporation had ceased to represent the most forward business men of the town, opposition grew as industry advanced. Thus the old rivalry of gentlemanly whig and gentlemanly tory had gone for ever, to be replaced by a more searching and bitter hostility, between old-fashioned defenders of Altar and Throne and the new radical school, who appeared to old whigs, as to tories, to be 'a set of drivellers . . . in their religion intolerable atheists, in their politics bloody-minded republicans, and in morals somewhat gross, and most selfish latitudinarians '.[2]

The liberal opposition in Leicester, aided by its newspapers, the *Chronicle* and Phillips's *Herald*, and with centres of propaganda in local chapels and in the Mechanics' Institute, grew remarkably between 1790 and its final triumph in 1835. Its influence became increasingly obvious in the parliamentary life of the borough, and culminated in the radical triumph of 1832. There are signs, however, that the opposition was slow to realize the implications of changed circumstances. Thus, in the election of 1790, the support of whig gentlemen of the county was still sought;[3] and when, owing to the violence of the contest, two candidates withdrew, the two members returned for the town, Thomas Boothby Parkyns, later Lord Rancliffe, for the opposition, and Samuel Smith, the banker, for the corporation interest, were both of them supporters of Pitt.[4] It

---

[1] Holt, op. cit. 4; journeymen were excluded by the rules of the Institute.

[2] Brougham's phrase, quoted by A. Aspinall, *Lord Brougham and the Whig Party* (1927), 145; compare also the interesting comment of Lord Holland to Lord Grey in 1826, 'Political parties are no more . . . the divisions of classes and great interests are arrayed against each other ', quoted by K. G. Feiling, op. cit. 401–2.

[3] *Leicester Journal*, 18 June 1790; Parkyns and Montolieu had in their support Booth Grey, Clement Winstanley, Walter Ruding, John Pares, and other whigs celebrated in the county.

[4] *Rutland Papers*, iii. 198. Smith, through his brother Robert, member for Nottingham, had a family link with the Rutland connexion; in 1807 he pre-

was not until the by-election of 1800, necessitated by the
death of Rancliffe, that the changed character of political
rivalries in Leicester became at all obvious. Then the
Leicester Journal gave expression to the view that now the
struggle was not, as it had been heretofore, merely between
'high' and 'low' parties, but 'between loyalty to the Constitution and Jacobinical Principles'.[1] Yet even now, the
candidate put forward by the opposition was a Manners.[2]
Although the corporation was successful in securing the
return to parliament of its candidate, Thomas Babington,
the poll for Manners was ominously large, and it was
claimed that at the close of the poll he had still many
voters to bring forward.[3] The value of the old-fashioned
electoral assets of birth and of landed property was shown
in 1802, when the radicals put forward a literary man, Felix
M'Carthy, without these assets, to stand in their interest,
and this candidate secured only a small poll.[4] None the
less, it was highly significant that the radicals should put
forward a candidate, standing entirely on their own bottom.

After the death of Pitt there were, for reasons not
altogether clear,[5] dissensions amongst the tories of Leicester,
which showed themselves in the election of 1807. Macnamara again appeared in the town as a candidate, to be
now opposed by the corporation, but supported by the
Journal.[6] These quarrels between the tories of the *Journal*

sented a portrait of Pitt to the corporation, see HB. 29 Oct. 1807. At the
close of the poll the voting was: Parkyns 986, Smith 803, Hallhead 551,
Montolieu, 551. See H. Stooks Smith, *Parliaments of England,* i (1844), 192.
In the violence of this election, a good many of the town archives were destroyed.
See also *Leicester Journal,* 2 and 9 July 1790. Parkyns (now Rancliffe) and
Smith were re-elected at the contested election of 1796, when the defeated election
candidates were Bertie Greathead and Walter Ruding.

[1] *Leicester Journal,* 5 Dec. 1800.
[2] Cf. Oldfield, *Representative History,* iv. 127; John Manners was supported
by his brother Sir William Manners, 'who had great property in the town and
neighbourhood'.
[3] *Leicester Journal,* loc. cit.: Manners 1,418, Babington 1,572. *The Times,*
20 Dec. 1800, 3 a.
[4] Stooks Smith, op. cit. i. 193: Babington 1,169, Smith 893, M'Carthy 333. *The
Times,* 8 July 1802, 3 c. M'Carthy was proposed by 'Mr. Brewin a Tanner'.
[5] Tentatively it may be suggested that the original union of the more conservative politicians had been largely based on personal devotion to Pitt, and so
was weakened for the time by Pitt's death.
[6] *Leicester Journal,* 15 May 1807; it was complained that Smith had dallied

and those of the corporation boded ill for the future of tory ascendancy at Leicester. Still more ominously, at the election of 1812 a plebeian group of extreme radicals, calling themselves 'the Friends of Peace Reform and Religious Liberty', put forward as their candidate a well-known reformer, an opponent of the slave-trade and a promoter of catholic emancipation, in the historian William Roscoe, formerly member for Liverpool.[1] In the middle of the war with Napoleon, at a time of grave domestic unrest, these friends of peace and reform had little hope of success. But they were led by a young bank clerk, Thomas Paget, who was within little more than twenty years to have the leading part in the final overthrow of the old corporation.

Finally, the election of 1818 had consequences of the greatest importance for the fortunes of the tory party in Leicester. The corporation permitted the return unopposed of two members, one for its own interest, in alderman John Mansfield, a local banker,[2] and the other for the opposition in Thomas Pares,[3] whose nomination was seconded by that pillar of radical nonconformity John Coltman.[4] The corporation thought of Pares as a conservative whig; but the *Journal*, doubting Pares's professions, remarked on the unwisdom of trusting any child of man. No preparations such as the enrolling of freemen had been made for the election by the corporation; Mansfield had conducted underhand intrigues to displace Smith;[5] and in fact, 'the

---

with reforming notions and been actually censured for this by the common hall, whereas Macnamara had steadfastly set his face against all innovation. As Macnamara was counted a whig and Smith a tory (cf. Stooks Smith, loc. cit.), this reflects the general meaninglessness at this time of these party labels.

[1] *Leicester Journal*, 9 Oct. 1812; Roscoe was proposed by 'a person of the name of BAILEY, *a cobbler or shoemaker* in Church Gate', and seconded by 'JONATHAN ATHERSTONE, a *dyer* in the town'; the poll was for Smith 1,116, Babington 967, Roscoe 412 (Stooks Smith, loc. cit.). For Roscoe, see *D.N.B.* xlix. 222–5.

[2] See Billson, *Leicester Memoirs*, 6–15.

[3] Ibid. 16–26; Pares's bank was started by John, the father of Thomas Pares, M.P.

[4] *Leicester Journal*, 12 June 1818.

[5] Ibid. 24 and 31 July 1818; Price, printer of the *Journal*, reports that at the common hall for discussing nominations Smith had 10 and Babington 28 votes. Smith left Leicester, disgusted at corporate ingratitude, while Babington feared to face a contest. There is also evidence that the members,

Opposition, by superior generalship, surprised the sentinels of THE BODY, whilst napping at their posts'.[1] Thomas Pares, so far from being a constitutional whig, turned out to be a middle-class reformer. He supported proposals so obnoxious to the tories of Leicester as parliamentary reform and catholic emancipation. But, though a radical, he refrained, significantly enough, from countenancing popular liberty, where this might threaten property.[2] That he retained his seat till 1826 was evidence that the corporation as a defender of 'church and king' toryism was little use. Since the two members, on crucial issues, usually voted on opposite sides, indignant tories complained that the town was virtually disfranchised.[3]

The corporation was in fact foundering on the rock of private ambition and family squabbles. It suffered from excessive inbreeding.[4] The election of Pares greatly increased radical influence in Leicester, at the expense of the corporation's prestige. Especially after 1822, with the liberalizing of Liverpool's ministry, obscurantists like the tories of the Leicester corporation were under a cloud; and it is significant that from 1822 the radical opponent in Leicester became most aggressive, and worked out ways of harassing the corporation that it pursued to the end. In 1822 the radicals exploited the plan for improvement commissioners in order to expose municipal abuses;[5] in 1823 they led complaints at the uselessness of the town grammar school, the headmaster, Richard Davies, having lost his memory;[6] and in the same year the agitators even enjoyed the corporation's support in an attack on the administration of Wigston's hospital, which only brought down on the common hall a severe snub from the duchy

especially Babington, had been unpopular for their lukewarm support of the framework knitters in their plight, see ibid. 22 May and 5 June 1818; for the corporation's sympathy with them see above, pp. 74–7.

[1] *Leicester Journal*, 12 June 1818.

[2] *The Black Book*, i (1820), 436; Pares voted for Burdett's motion of 1 July 1819; ii (1823), 182, he supported various reforming measures, but did not vote for repeal of the six acts or for the Manchester inquiry, or in 1822 for the reduction of the army and the influence of the Crown.

[3] *Leicester Journal*, 3 and 10 Mar. 1820.

[4] See list of members below, pp. 154–8.   [5] See above, pp. 33–5.

[6] Billson, *Leicester Memoirs*, 82; Cowie, op. cit. 98–9.

of Lancaster;[1] in 1824 and in 1825 there were attacks on the magistrates' policy of building a new jail,[2] and the corporation's management of Sir Thomas White's charity.[3] It was clear where the most vigorous political life was in Leicester; and that it was not in the weak and divided corporation.[4] Even the defence of toryism was left largely to the *Leicester Journal*.

The corporation, almost as unpopular with its friends as with its enemies, was thus in great need of rehabilitation. Out of this need came almost the last of its great electoral triumphs, in the next general election, that of 1826.[5] This was a Pyrrhic victory, fruitful only in disasters. The corporation was able to exploit the catholic question, which had been revived in 1820 and was of necessity a principal issue in the next ensuing general election. By strongly declaring opposition to all concessions to papists,[6] the corporation might hope to heal its own internal factions, defeat the radical enemy, and so restore its prestige as defender of church and state. Further, many nonconformists might be relied on to rise to a protestant cry, so that the leaders of the radical opposition in Leicester, chiefly unitarian supporters of catholic relief, would be deprived of a good deal of support. The Leicester corporation also fully understood that catholic emancipation must necessarily lead to the admission of protestant dissenters to an equality with churchmen in civic and political life. Thus the tories' municipal predominance in Leicester might be seriously threatened.

In order to gain the greatest local advantage for its cause from this unusually convenient national issue, the corporation began as early as December 1822 to create tory votes by the offer of the freedom to gentlemen of known constitutional principles, wherever these could be

---

[1] HB. 30 Dec. 1822; 3 Mar., 25 Apr., 6 Aug. 1823; PRO. DL 41/87; *Leicester Journal*, 29 Nov., 27 Dec. 1822, 3 Jan., 25 Apr., 22 Aug. 1823.

[2] See above, pp. 40–1.   [3] See above, p. 89.

[4] *Leicester Journal*, 12 June 1818, 3 Mar. 1820.

[5] A more detailed account of this election and its background is given in Greaves, R. W., 'Roman Catholic Relief in the Leicester Election of 1826', *Transactions of the Royal Historical Society*, 4th series, xxii (1940), 199–223.

[6] HB. 11 Apr. 1821, 22 May 1822 ; petitions against the measure.

found willing. This mode of preparation was carried on more systematically than ever before, and begun thus early in part to evade the Durham Act of 1763. In all some eight hundred freemen were enrolled, of whom some hundred were clergymen, known by the radicals as 'chaplains of the Holy Alliance'.[1] More difficulty was experienced by the corporation, in finding a candidate brave enough to face the expense and violence of a contested election, in which religious passions would certainly be highly inflamed. Doubt was even expressed of the capacity of the once powerful corporation to return even one candidate to S. Stephen's.[2] Thus there were two candidates already in the field before any could be brought forward in the old tory interest. First was a noted reformer, William Evans, a cotton-manufacturer who had been member for Retford in the previous parliament. He announced his intention of exposing the Leicester corporation in all its iniquity, should he be elected.[3] Next was a Canningite tory, Robert Otway Cave, from an old Leicestershire tory family, an owner of considerable estates in Ireland. While Evans was an outspoken supporter of the Roman catholic claims, Cave was as yet equivocal.[4] At long last, after much agitation, the Leicester tories found a candidate totally hostile to any whittling down of Anglican privilege, in Sir Charles Abney Hastings of Willersley hall.[5] His cause was unreservedly commended by a letter from the town clerk to the honorary freemen.[6]

Still there was a difficulty. Only one candidate was committed to opposing catholic emancipation; and the excellent results of the canvass for Evans showed how good a chance there was of success for the radicals. Consequently an alliance was concluded between the committees of the corporation, Cave, and Hastings. Cave was promised corporation help in return for his paying an

[1] HB. (according to an order of hall of 18 Dec. 1822), 30 Dec. 1822, 20 Jan. 1823, 3 Sept. 1824; Hartopp, *Register*, II. x–xiii; *The Times*, 21 June, 2 e, 21 June 1826, 3 b; Read, op. cit. 232; Hansard, N.S. xvi. 1198–1218; MCR. 1910 ff.   [2] *Leicester Journal*, 12 May 1826.
[3] Read, op. cit. 222; *The Black Book*, i (1820), 154; Gardiner, ii. 627–8.
[4] *Leicester Journal*, 12 May 1826.   [5] Ibid. 26 May 1826.
[6] MCR. 1910.

equitable share of the expenses, and for his promise that he would support corn-law repeal but abstain from voting in favour of catholic relief.[1] This alliance took outward shape in the close juxtaposition by the returning officer of voting-pens for Cave and Hastings, with one at a distance for Evans, votes being taken in rotation from each, so that Denman, a radical passing through Leicester, was called in as a second opposition candidate, in order to redress the balance. As a retort to this, Burbidge face- tiously proposed Cobbett and Hunt.[2]

The corporation's efforts had a successful outcome. Hastings and Cave were elected by respectable, though not by enormous, majorities.[3] For all the importance of the outvoters, it was found that the town voters were as a whole opposed to concessions to the papists.[4] Of the honorary freemen, little more than half voted,[5] so that the corporation derived greater advantage from 'the par- tiality of the returning officer, the unfairness of the over- seers, and the violence of the constables '.[6]

The victory, won by intimidation, bribery, and the worst form of religious prejudice, turned out to be in the end worse than any defeat. It left a legacy of financial difficulty, which was all the greater because Cave refused to pay £4,000 demanded of him by the corporation as still due from him for his share of expenses. This debt gave rise to heated altercations which turned Cave into an enemy of the corporation, and by their publicity were admirable propaganda for the reformers.[7] It was indeed the fact that 'in the Leicester Market, "No Popery" was an expensive article ',[8] for the total election expenses of

---

[1] MCR. 1910–11 ; Hansard, N.S. xvi. 1202.

[2] *The Times*, 15, 17, and 19 June 1826, 2 c, 4 b, 3 c respectively ; Hansard, N.S. xvi. 1204 ; Read, op. cit. 247.   Read mentions only the nomination of Cobbett.

[3] Poll Book (1826) : Hastings 2,773, Cave 2,678, Evans 2,063, Denman 1,811.   Stooks Smith, op. cit. i. 193.

[4] Hansard, N.S. xx. 358 ; Poll Book gives of town votes Hastings 1,211, Cave 1,105, Evans 1,098, Denman 953.

[5] MCR. 1910 ; Hartopp, *Register*, II. xiii.   [6] MCR. 1912–14.

[7] HB. 17 Sept. 1827, 27 Aug. 1828 (failure of attempt at arbitration) ; MCR. 1910–11 (text of agreement and account of dispute) ; *Leicester Journal*, 24 and 31 Aug. 1827.   Hansard, N.S. xix. 1300.

[8] *Leicester Chronicle*, 25 Aug. 1827.

the four candidates amounted to about £60,000.[1] The heavy liabilities made necessary a comprehensive readjustment of corporation finances,[2] and finally the mortgaging of a portion of the town estate to a rich clergyman, Henry Palmer of Carlton Curlieu, in return for a loan of £10,000.[3] This transaction was additional grist to the radicals' mill. In 1826 the corporation overreached itself, and financial exhaustion weakened it until its dissolution.

Moreover, after 1826 the radical opposition redoubled their effort, in a campaign of exposure conducted both in Leicester and in the commons. The corporation had, by its quarrel with Cave, supplied the opposition with a mouthpiece in parliament more belligerent than Pares had been. The administration of White's and Newton's charities, the expenditure of the borough rate, and the building of the town jail were all brought before the commons by the energetic Cave,[4] so that Peel complained that the house was being made an accessory to a petty local feud.[5] Cave's propaganda, together with the faults of other corporations, powerfully promoted the Corporate Funds Bill, of which he became the sponsor. The idea of an act to prevent municipal corporations from using corporate funds to influence parliamentary elections apparently originated with the defeated Leicester candidate Evans.[6] The bill at last became law in 1832;[7] as passed, it included provision against such transactions as that which the Leicester corporation had concluded with the Rev. Henry Palmer.[8]

Finally, the corporation's efforts were proved ineffectual to prevent the election of a Leicester member favourable to Roman catholic relief. Cave went over completely to the

---

[1] Gardiner, iii. 13–14.   [2] HB. 21 Mar., 27 Aug. 1828.

[3] HB. 17 Sept. 1827 (investment committee empowered to borrow); 24 Mar. 1829, the loan to be used in paying off sums borrowed on the security of some members of the corporation; MCR. 1902.

[4] Hansard, N.S. xix. 1649, 3rd series xx. 390–1; *Leicester Journal*, May–July 1828.

[5] Hansard, N.S. xix. 1762.

[6] Gardiner, ii. 628; *The Times*, 15 Dec. 1832, 1 d; F. Palgrave, in *House of Commons, Accounts and Papers*, 1835 (4), 9.

[7] Statute 2 & 3 Will. IV, c. 69; *HCJ*. lxxxvii, introduced by Evans, 17, 542.

[8] Statute 2 & 3 Will. IV, c. 69, § 3.

radical programme of civil and religious liberty. He voted
for the repeal of the civic disabilities of protestant dissenters
in 1828.[1] Above all, even before Wellington and Peel had
in face of a serious situation in Ireland 'retreated' on the
catholic issue,[2] Cave had declared himself in support of
emancipation.[3] He introduced into the house of commons
radical petitions from Leicester in favour of the measure,[4]
and gave his vote for it in the critical division.[5] Thus the
radicals of Leicester might regard with the utmost satisfaction the discomfiture of the corporation. It was observed
that the contest of 1826 had 'at least the merit of driving
several nails into the coffin' of the unreformed corporation.[6]
'The corporation, in debts and difficulties inextricable, are
becoming politically powerless.'[7]

[1] *Leicester Journal*, 7 and 28 Mar., 9 May 1828; HB. 21 Mar. 1828. The
Leicester corporation petitions against this measure.

[2] Cf. R. Peel, *Memoirs*, i (1856), 284–310.

[3] *Leicester Journal*, 5 Dec. 1828.

[4] Hansard, N.S. xx. 358, 701, 702; arguing that the Leicester electorate
now desired concessions to Roman catholics.

[5] Ibid. 1634.   [6] Read, op. cit. 247.

[7] *The Times*, 15 Sept. 1827, 3 a.

VIII

THE OPPONENT'S VICTORY, 1830–6

THE weakness of the corporation after 1826 was plainly shown by the events of 1830–2. In these years tories and churchmen, such as those of the Leicester corporation, were alarmed, even more than they had been by the reliefs given in 1828 and 1829 to protestant nonconformists and to Roman catholics, by the success of the campaign for parliamentary reform. Reform projects had been most enthusiastically sponsored by infidels and dissenters; propaganda writings like Wade's *Black Books* appealed equally to free-thinkers and to nonconformists. Naturally, therefore, reform was understood to mean the coming to power of dissenting tradespeople and factory-owners, who would attack the church of England. 'National apostasy' was a spectre closely present to the minds of churchmen, though it appeared in the attractive guise of 'civil and religious liberty' to the reformers.[1]

Even in this crisis the Leicester corporation was too exhausted by the contest of 1826 to risk the labour and expense of fighting an election in 1830, so that the old compromise of parties was restored. Cave having withdrawn,[2] the tory Hastings and the reformer Evans were returned as members for Leicester,[3] Evans still announcing his determination to press on with the Corporate Funds Bill.[4] The events of the next year were still more eloquent of municipal weakness. When in April 1831, in effect to delay constitutional deadlock, the king dissolved parliament, and a new election took place, fought solely on the ministry's plan of parliamentary reform, even then the Leicester corporation could do nothing. The two members returned for Leicester, Evans and

---

[1] For doubts felt even by members of Grey's ministry, C. Seymour, *Electoral Reform in England and Wales* (1915), 43.

[2] *Leicester Chronicle*, 28 Feb. and 31 July 1830; the liberals were divided in their opinions about Cave; ibid. 8 Aug. 1830, reports that Matthew Babington, a former tory, deprecated Cave's standing 'as being likely to weaken and endanger the independent interest of the town'.

[3] *Leicester Journal*, 6 Aug. 1830.

[4] Ibid. 4 Feb. 1831.

Wynn Ellis, were both of them reformers.[1] The Leicester
return was of a piece with the reforming triumph in all
parts of the country.

During the winter it became obvious that the only hope
of the obstructionist party was the house of lords. Consequently in September 1831,[2] and again in March 1832,
the corporation, by petition, called upon the upper house
to prevent the revolutionary changes proposed. Ignoring
such painful incidents as the recent peasants' revolt, the
corporation believed that existing institutions conferred
manifold benefits on all classes; it also affirmed that the
house of commons did not represent the sense of the
country, since gentlemen of correct principles 'were not
found to do their duty to the Country by standing forward
as candidates'; and it feared that the democratic tendency
of the measure threatened all that was valuable and venerable. 'Neither our readings nor our experience teach us
to love Democratic Rule.' 'The true liberties of the
people . . . never did, and never will, long survive the
wreck of the Throne and the Altar.'[3] The corporation
most despairingly was trying to stem the tide. On 7 June
1832 the Reform Bill became law.[4]

The changes in the English parliamentary system made
by the Reform Act of 1832 and its satellites the Boundaries
Act and the Corporate Funds Act, though hardly so productive of 'democratic rule' as the Leicester common
hall so mistakenly assumed, certainly revolutionized the
conditions of party conflict in most towns, particularly
where the municipal corporations had had great influence.
The old franchise at Leicester had been relatively democratic, and the immediate effect of the enfranchisement of
'the solid and intelligent class' of £10 householders was
not seriously to alter the number of town votes.[5] The
great change was in the elimination of the outvoters, the

---

[1] *Leicester Journal*, 11 Nov. 1831, 18 May 1832; they had been supported
by a political union.

[2] HB. 29 Sept. 1831.   [3] HB. 29 Mar. 1832.

[4] Statute 2 Will. IV, c. 45.

[5] The number of town votes cast in 1826 was 4,372. Read, op. cit. 261,
states that in 1832 out of a population of 40,512 there were 1,769 voters;
4,456 votes were cast in the December election.

constituency being by this reduced by half.[1] This change
tended to favour the local liberals, for the corporation
could no longer enrol as freemen for election purposes
non-resident tories, and also, the liberals found in local
chapels useful centres of organization. Further benefit
was conferred on the liberal interest by the Boundaries
Act, which extended the parliamentary borough to include
the 'new borough',[2] though this was to some extent offset
by the continuance of the resident freemen's franchise, so
long as they should live.[3] Lastly, a most important change
was effected by the reform, in the introduction into the
town of the whole apparatus of registration of voters.[4]

The election of 1832, fought under these new conditions,
was a triumph for the reformers, at Leicester as it was in
most other places. Evans and Wynn Ellis were elected
by good majorities.[5] For the first time since 1768 the
corporation in a straight fight was completely beaten. The
London *Times* characteristically observed that the corporation had 'much reason to lament the disfranchisement of
non-residents, as they have thereby lost the assistance of
the vast proportion of the 800 honorary freemen, whom
they had so unblushingly called into existence to stifle the
fair expression of popular opinion'; nor 'had they any
cause to rejoice in the passing of the Corporate Funds
Bill'.[6] Indeed, the Corporate Funds Act was the greater
advantage to the liberals, because it did not hinder individuals, as it did corporations, from using their money in
bribery, and there is good liberal evidence that the liberals,
as well as the tories, had a highly organized system of
treating.[7] The *Leicester Herald*, now ultra-tory, went so

[1] Seymour, op. cit. 84.

[2] Statute 2 & 3 Will. IV, c. 64, schedule O, section 20 ; *Leicester Chronicle*,
1 Dec. 1832. The act specified for the parliamentary borough of Leicester ' the
Old Borough of Leicester and the Space over which the Magistrates of the Old
Borough of Leicester at present exercise Jurisdiction concurrently with the
Magistrates of the County of Leicester, including the Castle View'.

[3] Statute 2 Will. IV, c. 45, §§ 32–3.   [4] Ibid. §§ 27–8, 44–7.

[5] *Leicester Journal*, 14 Dec. 1832: the poll was calculated as follows : Evans
1,682, Ellis 1,538, Leigh 1,276. They had had the support of a Political
Union, MCR. 1897. Read, op. cit. 261, gives slightly different figures.

[6] *The Times*, 15 Dec. 1832, 1 d.

[7] *House of Commons, Reports of Committees*, 1835 (4), committee on bribery,
§§ 2120 ff., evidence of James Hudson, a liberal manufacturer of Leicester, to

far as to declare that reform had 'introduced unblushing
venality' into Leicester, and that poor voters had been
offered £3 a head to vote in the liberal interest.[1] But
probably the liberals' most effective weapon was their
superior understanding of the all-important technique of
registration.[2]

The reformers' success in the general election of 1832
meant that drastic changes would be made in town government. As Cobbett saw, parliamentary reform of necessity
led to municipal reform. The legal admission of dissenters
to a normal membership of corporations in 1828 and the
Corporate Funds Act of 1832 were simply preludes to a
municipal revolution. In 1832 Grey's government made
a start on the Scotch boroughs.[3] In the February of 1833
a select committee of the commons was set up to investigate English, Welsh, and Irish municipal corporations,
but this, finding the whole subject too vast and intricate,
recommended instead the appointment of a royal commission to make a detailed survey. This commission was finally
set up in July 1833. It consisted for England and Wales
of some twenty young barristers of radical leanings. They
had about eighteen months in which to prepare their
report. In order to cover the ground, they divided themselves in pairs, along lines suggested by the select committee's report, each pair taking a selected number or
circuit of boroughs. In all, these young lawyers examined
witnesses and records in over two hundred and eighty
towns.[4] On 14 September 1833 Whitcombe and Cockburn,
the commissioners for the north midland circuit, arrived
at Leicester, to begin their investigation there.[5]

They found the town in a fever of political excitement,
aggravated by recent events. Earlier in the year the corporation had successfully prosecuted for criminal libel the

the effect that in the elections of 1826, 1832, and 1835 both parties treated
extensively. Hudson was elected a councillor of the reformed corporation.

[1] *Leicester Herald*, 19 Dec. 1832.
[2] Cf. for the opinion of Lord Palmerston on the importance of registration,
The Early Correspondence of Lord John Russell, ii. 72 (Palmerston to Russell,
22 Jan. 1835).
[3] Statute 3 & 4 Will. IV, c. 76 (1833).
[4] *ELG.* iii. 710–16; *Annual Register, 1833* (1834), Chronicle, 341.
[5] *Leicester Journal*, 20 Sept. 1833.

author and printer of a pamphlet which severely criticized
the administration of justice and the use of public funds
at Leicester;[1] about the time of the commissioners' arrival
the corporation was organizing a drive against non-free
beer-sellers, in virtue of a favourable decision it had
secured in King's Bench;[2] and the radicals had busied
themselves in instigating in the commons inquiry into the
use of White's loan money.[3] In these circumstances, it
was particularly noticeable that on the night of their
arrival the commissioners dined at the house of Robert
Brewin (a radical so definite as to support the ballot), in
company with the great enemy of the corporation Thomas
Paget, the dissenting minister Berry, the leading radical
lawyer Stone, and some others of the same party.[4]

The next day the inquiry began. It was held, by
courtesy of the county magistrates, at the castle, with the
result that the proceedings were public.[5] The corporation
plainly regarded the commission as a hostile body. A
month before, the hall had empowered a committee appointed originally to deal with the libellous pamphlet to
deal with this new menace also.[6] But to all intents and
purposes the committee counted little. The important
person was Thomas Burbidge, the town clerk. The corporation was totally at his mercy. 'The terms are synony-
mous . . . the Town Clerk is their master.'[7] Though
there was much that Burbidge was only too anxious to
conceal, the attitude adopted by the corporation under his
guidance was not, like that of five other bodies, sheer
refusal of all information,[8] although he held the view common amongst extreme tories that the commission was un-
constitutional.[9] The first part of the inquiry was taken up
by the examination of Burbidge and a group of radical

[1] *Leicester Journal*, 26 Apr., 10 May 1833; HB. 1 Apr. 1833. The defendants
were Thompson, printer of the *Chronicle*, and Cockshaw, a printer who sold the
pamphlet. Evans introduced the pamphlet as a petition in the commons.
[2] HB. 19 Aug. 1833.
[3] Hansard, 3rd series, xx. 390–1, 6 Aug. 1833.
[4] *Leicester Journal*, 20 Sept. 1833.
[5] *Leicester Chronicle*, 14 Sept. 1833.   [6] HB. 19 Aug. 1833.
[7] *Leicester Chronicle*, 28 Sept. 1833.   [8] *ELG.* iii. 717 n. 2.
[9] *Leicester Journal*, 11 Oct. 1833; cf. Hansard, 3rd series, xxvi. 314–16, for
Lyndhurst's opinion.

witnesses. According to Burbidge, he first sought permission to consult the recorder about the propriety of his
divulging information, in a public meeting, that he had
obtained in his confidential capacity of town clerk. This
permission the commissioners refused, since such information was really what they wanted. Following this, Burbidge
answered questions about the corporation, its constitution,
income and expenditure, apparently satisfactorily.[1] According to the *Chronicle*, the most striking facts to be
revealed were the offering of the freedom to two thousand
persons before the election of 1826, and the mortgaging
of corporation property after it. The former of these
measures was justified as the outcome of 'a desire to maintain the principles . . . thought best calculated to promote
the good of the country'; the latter on the ground that
the land mortgaged had been bought in the reign of
Elisabeth by individual members out of their own pockets,
and was therefore the private property of the present corporation 'and not that of the public at large'.

After Burbidge, a number of radicals were called,
including Paget, Brewin, Cockshaw, and Coltman.[2] Burbidge objected to their evidence as 'improper' and was
allowed to call witnesses of his own. Attention was now
concentrated on the partiality of the magistrates,[3] and a
counter-declaration was signed by eight hundred householders of confidence in the magistracy.[4]

At the beginning of the second week of the inquiry,
corporation and commissioners openly quarrelled. The
commissioners demanded that the town clerk should sur-
render to them the hall books for the last twenty, and the
chamberlains' accounts for the last ten, years, and a variety
of other documents, 'embracing the minutest details of
corporation affairs', especially titles to land, drafts of mort-
gages and other securities, as well as particulars of payments to the corporation.[5] Burbidge offered to convey
these documents to the commissioners' lodgings, on con-

[1] HB. 24 Sept. 1833; Burbidge's report to the common hall.
[2] *Leicester Chronicle*, 21 Sept. 1833.
[3] *Leicester Journal*, 27 Sept. 1833, with editorial comments.
[4] *Leicester Chronicle*, 21 Sept. 1833; MCR. 1922 n.
[5] HB. 24 Sept. 1833, Burbidge's report.

dition that they were confined to their own inspection, a promise of privacy which they refused to give, on the ground that outside evidence might be needed to illuminate the documents.[1] The commissioners had also refused to allow Burbidge to consult the recorder on a question of a title to property. It was therefore an easy conclusion for persons in the position of the members of the corporation to draw, that the object of the inquiry was not to ascertain the truth, but to hold up the body to 'the obloquy and illwill of their political opponents'. Another reason for refusal that could be alleged was emphasized by Burbidge, namely, the general excitement at the meetings at the castle. The town clerk's vivid report produced just the effect he wished. The corporation refused to allow the documents required to be delivered to the commissioners,[2] and persisted in this refusal in spite of the commissioners' assurances that their meetings were orderly and that publicity given to papers was not excessive.[3]

The corporation in fact carried the war into the enemy's camp. In a widely published announcement the common hall attacked the commissioners' claims both to impartiality and to legality. All papers submitted were used solely to assail the property and character of the corporation. The commissioners, in the corporation's opinion, possessed no right in law to call public meetings, least of all meetings that provoked public irritation by reviving the memories of battles past.[4] This attack on the lawfulness of the proceedings so incensed Whitcombe that he threatened to treat it as a libel on the house of commons,[5] but he was obliged in the end to concede that the corporation had every right to withhold what it thought fit. After hearing a few more witnesses, chiefly on the 1826 election and on the sales of lands in the south field, Whitcombe and Cockburn departed to worry the castle-ridden corporation of Warwick. 'O iam satis!' exclaimed the tory *Journal* at their departure.[6]

---

[1] *Leicester Journal*, 11 Oct.; *Leicester Chronicle*, 28 Sept. 1833.
[2] HB. 24 Sept. 1833.
[3] *Leicester Chronicle*, 28 Sept. 1833.   Cf. MCR. 1885–9.
[4] HB. 17 Oct. 1833.   [5] *Leicester Journal*, 11 Oct. 1833.
[6] Ibid. 18 Oct. 1833.

This was not the end of the corporation's dealings with the inquiry. In the following March an account was sent to the commission: of local charities, of freemen admitted, and of corporation charters, but chiefly of the sales of corporation property and the uses to which the purchase money was put. It was intended to show that, while between £17,000 and £18,000 had been raised since 1814 by sales of land,[1] over £20,000 had been spent in 'purchases and in beneficial improvements of the Corporation property and for public purposes as specified'. This information, the corporation submitted, would be found 'the best practical answer to the insinuations so liberally made against the Corporation that they had sold largely from the Corporation Estates and had spent or embezzled the purchase moneys'.[2]

It was, of course, loudly proclaimed by the liberals' papers, and as loudly denied by tory writers, that the corporation had disgraced itself in the inquiry.[3] It was, moreover, asserted that the corporation had been divided on the subject of refusing information to the commissioners.[4] Indeed, we may conclude that responsibility for the breach rests on both sides. The commissioners, hand in glove with the radical opposition, were not accommodating, and must have seemed to the tories of the town to be youthful, arrogant, and prejudiced. On the other hand, the corporation, long accustomed to complete autonomy, resented the interference of this commission and hated the newfangled appeal to a vociferous public. It no doubt felt that in giving any information at all it was behaving with an extreme liberality.

The work of the commissioners in preparing their report was not interrupted by the transitory tory revival that marked the latter part of 1834. Much more than the municipal commissioners, the threat to the church stimulated tory partisanship into action. Clergy and laity banded together in associations to defend the church from the on-

---

[1] For sales since 1810 see above, p. 86.
[2] HB. 24 Mar. 1834; cf. MCR. 1902–7.
[3] *Leicester Chronicle*, 5 Oct. 1833, and *passim*; *Leicester Journal*, 18 Oct. 1833.
[4] *Leicester Chronicle*, 12 Oct. 1833.

slaughts of a secularizing liberalism.[1] The modest proposals of the ministry of Grey for reducing the number of
Irish bishoprics, and the abortive tithe bill of 1834, seemed
to many a prelude to a general attack on the church in
the interests of papists, dissenters, and infidels.[2] Melbourne's hesitation in face of this problem led to the
'hundred days' of tory rule under Wellington and Peel.
It was during the 'hundred days' that the next general
election took place, in January 1835. It was dominated
everywhere by the church question. 'The church in danger'
was the cry raised by the corporation of Leicester.[3] It was
reiterated in the columns of the *Leicester Journal*.[4] The
danger of the church was stressed at the hustings.[5]

For the first time since 1812 the corporation saw the
return for Leicester of two candidates well affected to the
church. The liberals were at the bottom of the poll; Goulburn and T. Gladstone were elected.[6] An attempt to unseat Goulburn failed.[7] Under stress of the danger to the
Establishment, the 'conservatives', as they were now calling themselves, had applied their energies to the manipulation of the new electoral machinery. Magistrates and
clergymen brought pressure on parish officers to see that
tory voters were registered, as the act provided. The conservative societies, which had grown up during the previous decade, actively furthered the corporation party's
cause.[8] The defeated liberals complained also of the use

---

[1] S. C. Carpenter, *Church and People 1788–1888* (1933), 117–18.

[2] Cf. W. Palmer, *Narrative of Events connected with the Tracts for the Times*
(ed. 1883), 38. It is worth noting that even at Leicester there was a vicar of
S. Martin's who did not share the corporation's attitude, Andrew Erskine,
who forbade in 1834 the ringing of the bells at the corporation feast, holding
that the Church should not be subject to one political party. *Leicester Journal*,
13 and 30 June, 4 July 1834.   [3] HB. 10 June 1834.

[4] *Leicester Journal*, 22 Nov. 1833, 23 May 1834.   [5] Ibid. 2 Jan. 1835.

[6] Goulburn was recorder of Leicester. Stooks Smith gives as votes cast:
Goulburn 1,484, Gladstone 1,475, Evans 1,352, Ellis 1,314. Similarly Read,
op. cit. 261.

[7] The petition was on the ground that Goulburn lacked the necessary property
qualification. Its hearing was delayed by the town clerk's exploitation of
a technical error in the petition, but when this had been corrected the petition
was disallowed; Hansard, 3rd series, xxvii. 267–70, 464, 544; *Leicester Journal*,
3 Apr.; *Leicester Chronicle*, 4 Apr. 1835; *The Times*, 13 Jan. 1835, 4 d.

[8] *Leicester Journal*, 9 Jan. 1835, attributes the conservative victory to these
societies.

of government influence against them. For the tory candidates were 'the brother of a Cabinet minister, and the
brother of a member of the administration not in the
Cabinet.'[1] ... The Church, the Government, the Corporation, the tax-gatherer, the sexton, the grave-digger ... all,
high and low, who held place and power had been arrayed
against them, and had prevailed.'[2] It was also significant
that Burbidge, the town clerk, was as active in 1835 as he
had been in 1826. He later claimed to have paid out £233,
relating exclusively to journeys to London, on 'particular
business', in December 1834—the 'particular business'
being naturally taken by the reformed corporation to 'have
reference to the approaching general election'.[3] Burbidge
might well be active. The church of England was not in
so great jeopardy as the municipal corporations.

Though the conservative membership of the house of
commons was increased, it was still in a minority. Peel's
ministry therefore soon inevitably fell, and the Melbourne
party returned. Yet the brief 'hundred days' had made
the fall of the old corporations even more inevitable, for
in February and March, whigs and radicals in the Lich-
field house compact had agreed to co-operate against the
tory revival on a reforming platform.[4] Still more decisive
was the publication in March 1835 of the report on
municipal corporations. This must have been a final blow
to the tory revival. In general, the report was remarkable for precision, lucidity, and completeness. But it was
prefaced by a general introduction, which was simply a
rhetorical philippic against all corporations. This introduction was all that most people were likely to read of the
four formidable volumes produced by the commissioners.
As it was a work of propaganda much more than of science,
it fulfilled an important purpose of the whole investigation,
by stimulating the demand for reform.[5]

Lord John Russell's bill passed the commons with a

---

[1] H. Goulburn was home secretary; W. E. Gladstone (aet. 29) at the treasury.
[2] *Leicester Chronicle*, 17 Jan. 1835.
[3] MS. Council Minutes, 9 Nov. 1836.
[4] Spencer Walpole, *History of England from 1815* (ed. 1880), iii. 295-6.
[5] *ELG.* iii. 717-19; for the kind of language the report encouraged, see
H. Martineau, *History of England during the Thirty Years Peace* (1850), ii. 238.

surprising ease, in much the same form as his earliest
draft,[1] with the critical support of Peel,[2] who had advocated
municipal reform in the Tamworth manifesto.[3] Russell's
bill, in the form in which it passed the commons, preserved
none of the venerable inconsistencies so attractive to conservative sentiment, but sought to substitute for them a
utilitarian uniformity. All the 183 boroughs for which
the bill prescribed were to have elected town councils, the
councillors being elected for three years, one-third retiring
yearly. To these new bodies the rights and properties of
the old were transferred, together with the control of public
houses, policing and watching, and the power of levying
a borough rate. The municipal franchise proposed in this
bill was so democratic as to arouse Peel's strong dislike,
being vested in all ratepaying householders of three years'
residence. Freemen's pecuniary rights were preserved, but
trading privileges were abolished.[4]

In the lords the reformers had a struggle against wreck-
ing amendments, chiefly from Lyndhurst, the most vigorous
opponent of the measure. Lyndhurst persuaded the lords to
hear evidence at the bar on behalf of the corporations. The
corporations were represented at the bar by two lawyers,
Knight, a king's counsel, and the extraordinary Wetherall,
recorder of Bristol. Burbidge, who was with many other
town clerks up in London, lobbying peers and working
hard against the bill,[5] saw the value of this opportunity.
The common hall therefore instructed its finance committee, together with the justices, to take any steps necessary in this crisis, and to draw up a petition to be heard
at the bar of the house. The arguments of this petition
are worth notice. In the first place, the common hall
denounced the bill as bad, by reason of its origin in an

---

[1] *Early Correspondence of Lord John Russell*, ii. 110–12.

[2] Hansard, 3rd series, xxviii. 562–71; *Croker Papers* (ed. L. J. Jennings, 1884),
ii. 283; Greville, 14 June 1835, in *The Greville Memoirs* (ed. H. Reeve), iii
(1874), 263.

[3] *Annual Register for 1834* (1835), 341.   [4] *ELG*. iii. 738–41.

[5] MS. Council Minutes, 19 Aug. 1836; Burbidge claimed £884 for opposing
the Municipal Reform Act; £120 as a subscription to the general fund in London;
£525 for attendance in London; £92 for his clerks' journeys; £140. 5s. for
correspondence; and £12. 12s. for 'wrapping up, sealing, directing and sending
out three Letters'; £105 for his agent; totalling in all over £900.

unjust report. Second, in the three-year ratepaying qualification the bill was dangerously democratic. Third, an argument that their lordships would easily understand, the bill was an assault on property; for the existing corporations held their properties by titles not substantially different from those on which the peers held their own dignities and estates, so that the passage of the bill might easily create a very dangerous precedent, diminishing property and abrogating privileges protected by royal grants. Finally, with special reference to the estates of Gabriel Newton, who made his benefaction to the corporation as churchmen, it was 'a fraud of the gravest character' to hand over the Newton estates to 'others who may be and it is most likely will be of principles totally opposite to those which the Donor himself would have looked for'.[1]

The petition was received, and the representatives of the Leicester, as of certain other, corporations were heard.[2] It was found that the evidence of the corporations was not of value to the opponents of the Municipal Corporations Reform Bill.[3] Peel made it plain that he would not countenance Lyndhurst's policy of destruction and abet the upper house in a contest with the lower. Against continuing any of the existing members of corporations in their offices, simply because they were already there, Peel steadfastly set his face.[4] The act as finally passed included concessions to the tory opposition, which improved the measure without essentially changing it. The democratic franchise and the elected town councils were retained, but the right of licensing innkeepers was denied the new councils. As a concession to the tories, the office of alderman, in a revised form, was allowed to continue—the aldermen in the new dispensation to be appointed for six years by the councillors, one-half retiring triennially by rotation.[5] In spite of the anger of Roebuck, Place, and their friends at the modifications made in the original scheme,[6] the act as passed did provide the starting-point of a great extension

---

[1] HB. 24 July 1835.　　　　　　[2] *HLJ.* lxvii. 328, 389–400.
[3] *ELG.* iii. 743.　　　　[4] Ibid. 745–6.　　　　[5] Ibid. 747, 754.
[6] R. E. Leader, *Autobiography and Letters of J. A. Roebuck* (1897), 44, 69–71; G. Wallas, *Life of Francis Place* (1925), 341–6.

of municipal government.[1] From the point of view of contemporaries it was important that the steam-engine had now been provided to the mill built by parliamentary reform.[2]

The Municipal Corporations Reform Act, limited as it was in scope to some 178 larger towns, excluding the greatest of all corporations, that of the city of London, yet introduced into municipal life that device of a ratepayers' democracy, which had been applied only the year before with some differences to the administration of the poor law.[3] The revising barristers very quickly set to work, as provided by the act, in compiling the first registers of local electors, who were to be drawn for the municipal borough from the whole area covered by the new parliamentary constituency.[4] Registration was now as important a feature of local, as it was already of parliamentary, politics. It was pointed out that the battle to control the new town council would be fought in the registration courts.[5] The radical party tried to secure a disfranchisement of recipients of Sir Thomas White's loan money, under the clause excluding from the franchise those in receipt of poor relief, but this argument was rightly disallowed by the revising barristers.[6] At the same time the barristers had also to consider the division of the town into seven wards, as prescribed in the schedule of the act, and in doing this they followed the suggestion of Burbidge in keeping as far as possible the old boundaries.[7]

The stage was now set for the first municipal election in the history of Leicester. The two parties, conservatives and liberals, put forward their candidates. It was very noticeable that the conservative organization, the Central Constitutional Municipal Committee, put forward a very mixed collection of ' moderate whigs and temperate conservatives, churchmen and dissenters . . . nearly all that is estimable in Leicester for station, moderation, and

[1] See especially in the act 5 & 6 Will. IV, c. 76, §§ 76–86, 87–8.
[2] S. Reid, *Life and Letters of Lord Durham*, ii (1906), 72.
[3] Statute 4 & 5 Will. IV, c. 76, § 38.
[4] Statute 5 & 6 Will. IV, c. 76, §§ 7, 15–20, 28; *ELG.* iii. 749, n. 1.
[5] *Leicester Journal*, 30 Oct. 1835.   [6] Ibid. 4 Dec. 1835.
[7] Ibid. 16 and 23 Oct. 1835; Statute 5 & 6 Will. IV, c. 76, § 39.

intelligence'. It was still more noticeable that the conservative committee felt it necessary to point out that its candidates had 'no more to do with the old Corporation than with a company of dancing dervishes'.[1] Only ten of the old corporation were considered good enough to stand the ordeal of popular election, and only one of the last eight mayors.[2] These local events thus give a clear evidence of the necessity for Peel's new 'conservatism' if there was to be any counterblast to a triumphant liberalism. It was only by abandoning the old toryism of the unreformed corporation that the conservatives in Leicester might hope, as they did, for a moderate council, not dominated by the 'socinian faction'.[3] These hopes were in no way justified by the event. The liberals of the 'socinian faction' had a sweeping victory. Only four of the forty-two candidates of the conservative committee were elected; none of these had been a member of the old corporation.[4] This resounding defeat the conservatives attributed to apathy in their ranks, and the framing of the Reform Act in such a way as to make a conservative success impossible. Certainly, their defeat reflected the profound discredit now fallen on the old corporation.

The conservative cause had not been assisted by the last acts of the unreformed body, which, seeing that the end was near, made final distribution of large amounts of corporation funds. At the end of October the hall decided not to hold the corporation feast as usual, no doubt feeling that a fast more befitted its condition. By way of compensation the hall granted annuities to various of the corporation officials, amounting in all to nearly £500.[5] The next month it granted pieces of plate to the town clerk and two of the aldermen, totalling in value 450 guineas, the town clerk, true to character, taking the lion's share. The corporation's pipe of wine was voted to the Leicester infirmary, and the salaries of the mayor and various

---

[1] *Leicester Journal*, 25 Dec. 1835.
[2] *Leicester Chronicle*, 26 Dec. 1835.   [3] *Leicester Journal*, 18 Dec. 1835.
[4] Ibid. 1 Jan. 1836; the four conservative councillors were all elected in east S. Margaret's ward and were Joseph Philips, Charles Inman, George Lockwood, and William Miles. See below, p. 159.
[5] HB. 29 Oct. 1835.

officers were ordered to be paid to them for the current year.[1] On the eve of Christmas the companies met again. Finding that the gifts voted at the recent halls had been made 'a handle for doing injury to the general conservative cause', the town clerk, the two aldermen, and the steward came forward to decline what they had formerly accepted. The thanks of the hall were therefore voted to 'the several gentlemen who have made these sacrifices to public feeling and who have thereby manifested their devotion to the Conservative cause to be above any personal or pecuniary consideration'.[2]

This pathetic bravado was not quite the last act of the old corporation. Three days later, on the feast of S. John the Evangelist, the two companies attended, as was their wont, the charity sermon in aid of the widows of S. John's hospital.[3] The next day, at the close of the municipal election, the mayor, by declaring the results, was the principal minister of the old corporation's obsequies. For by the publishing, as the act directed, of the election results— so Burbidge recorded with flourishes and defiant underlinings—'by the 38th section of the said Act this Corporation which had existed from time immemorial was doomed to final DISSOLUTION. Nevertheless God save the king and all that are set in authority under *him*'.[4] Finally, after the election of aldermen, chosen as the act allowed by co-option from outside the ranks of the councillors just elected,[5] that notorious radical, the leader of the 'socinian faction', Thomas Paget, was elected and sworn in as the first mayor of the reformed municipality,[6] 'and thereupon the Head was placed upon this new Body and it then received its perfect corporate existence'.[7]

The worst fears of the old corporation were justified.

---

[1] HB. 22 Dec. 1835.   [2] HB. 24 Dec. 1835.   [3] HB. 27 Dec. 1835.

[4] HB., Burbidge's last entry, dated 1 Jan. 1836; reprinted in full in Hartopp, *Register*, II. xiv.

[5] Statute 5 & 6 Will. IV, c. 76, §§ 25, 27; *ELG*. iii. 754.

[6] For Paget's career see Billson, *Leicester Memoirs*, 32-3; in 1825, after some twenty-five years as a partner in Pares's bank, he set up the banking firm of Paget & Kirby. He represented the county in the parliament of 1831. As member for Leicestershire he spoke in favour of the Corporate Funds Bill; Hansard, 3rd series, iv. 405. He died in 1862 at the age of 84.

[7] HB. 1 Jan. 1836.

Principles totally opposite to their own were triumphing in the new corporations almost everywhere. Contemporary whigs regarded the municipal reform as 'a much greater blow to toryism than the Reform Bill itself'.[1] The historian of the dissenters held that the act achieved what the relieving legislation of 1828 had failed to do, for it proved 'the most effective practical repeal of the corporation act' of Charles II.[2] This issue of many years' conflict was particularly clear at Leicester. 'Of the 56 Aldermen and Councillors elected by the Town under the new Municipal Act', it was recorded by the new town council in 1837, 'more than two thirds are Dissenters of various denominations.'[3] The new mayor, the new town clerk,[4] and the six mayors next following were all members of the unitarian Great Meeting, which was in consequence known as the 'mayors' nest'.[5] The nineteenth-century ascendancy of nonconformity in Leicester was inaugurated.

The displacing from power, by Paget, Coltman, Brewin, Whetstone, and their friends, of the old tory corporation was yet even more than this victory of certain political and religious principles. The Municipal Corporations Reform Act immensely strengthened the position of a fairly clearly marked social class. It greatly favoured the substantial middle class.[6] The rule of the few old tory families that had dominated the unreformed corporation was now overthrown. The local government of the town was more broadly based. It was now safely in the hands of the leaders of the town's business community, men alienated by the nepotism, the

---

[1] *Creevey Papers*, ed. H. Maxwell (1903), ii. 308; cited *ELG*. iii. 750.

[2] J. Bennett, *History of the Dissenters during the Thirty Years 1808-38* (1839), 83.

[3] MS. Council Minutes, 25 Jan. 1837; it was significant that in Dec. 1835 three newly elected members refused to take the oath not to damage the established church imposed by 9 Geo. IV, c. 17, § 2, when this was offered to them by Burbidge according to 5 & 6 Will. IV, c. 76, § 50; these were councillor Thomas Burgess and aldermen W. E. Hutchinson and Samuel Waters. HB. 1 Jan. 1836; *Leicester Journal*, 1 Jan. 1836.

[4] Samuel Stone.

[5] *Centenary Book of the Great Meeting Schools 1783-1883*, 7-9.

[6] Statute 5 & 6 Will. IV, c. 76, §§ 9, 28. This latter clause established a property qualification for mayors and councillors of boroughs with four or more wards, of £1,000 real and personal estate, or payment of rate of £30 a year; less for smaller towns.

toryism, and even the economic measures of the old corporation.[1]

The changed complexion of the Leicester corporation was reflected in the first measures of the new council. The tory conviviality of the old common halls gave way to the more frugal, business-like exactitude of their nonconformist successors. At an early council meeting William Biggs and Robert Brewin, the one a hosier, the other a worsted-spinner, brought forward and carried a motion to sell by public auction the insignia that had dignified the functions of the old corporation, and as well the plate, crockery, and culinary utensils formerly needed on feasting days. At the same meeting it was decided that members of the public might be present at council meetings, by signed order from a member of the corporation.[2] The finance committee, soon after, recommended the abolition of the office of sergeant-at-mace, since the 'true dignity of the mayoralty does not consist in antiquated pageantry'; and as well suggested that 'an office of great antiquity but of little public utility . . . the Office of Mole Catcher may be abolished without any disadvantage to the Public Service'.[3] Still more significant of the changed régime, the council was unable to overcome the temptation to petition against the remaining nonconformist grievances, and especially against church rates.[4] The old high church toryism had been decisively excluded from the civic life of a municipality which had formerly been one of its strongholds.

Yet, even now, the more militant members of the old corporation were not quelled. When the new council, anxious to find exactly the financial position it had inherited,[5] applied to the officers and members of the late corporation for the hall books and accounts, these were refused. Only after much haggling were the hall books delivered.[6] It was not until they were needed to investigate

---

[1] See lists cited in Appendix, below, pp. 154-9.
[2] MS. Council Minutes, 4 Jan. 1836.   [3] Ibid. 13 Jan. 1836.
[4] Ibid. 20 and 24 May 1837; the council hesitated about supporting officially any specifically liberal measure, but in the end the aggressive party carried the day; 25 Jan. 1837, petition against church rates.
[5] Ibid. 1 Jan. 1836; appointment of finance committee.
[6] Ibid. 13 Jan. and 19 Aug. 1836; notwithstanding § 65 of the act.

the demands of Burbidge that the accounts from 1820 were handed over, and even then not all.   Most irritating were the impudent demands of the ex-town clerk.   Under the clause of the Municipal Reform Act which allowed to dispossessed officers of old corporations compensation for the loss of their employments, subject to their having been of good behaviour,[1] Burbidge claimed nearly £11,000. As he was 'indebted to the Corporation at the time of his removal from office in upwards of £10,000', it looks as if he found himself in a tight corner, and was claiming sufficient to cover his liabilities.[2]   The committee that examined Burbidge's claim reported caustically that 'a servant who has so conducted himself, who has received money and applied it to his own use, and who has refused to account for it to his employers, conduct which in inferior servants would have subjected them to a criminal prosecution, is not entitled to any compensation for his loss of office . . . the conduct of Burbidge fully justified the Council in dismissing him from the Public Service'.[3]

Burbidge was not the least abashed by such censures. He carried his case on appeal, as the Municipal Reform Act allowed, to the treasury.   There he was awarded in 1851 outrageously generous compensation, an annuity of £889. 3s. 6d. payable as from 1 January 1836 to his death. Only the expense of further battle prevented the corporation of Leicester from attempting to reverse this award. Burbidge, now an old man, was willing to compromise. In 1853 he concluded a bargain very advantageous to himself—unduly advantageous in view of his heavy defalcations.   He received £400 down, £200 for the year ending December 1853, and £600 yearly for the rest of his life. Two years later he died.[4]   With his death the history of the unreformed corporation of Leicester comes to its not very glorious end.   It had fought to the last, 'and may be said to have died kicking'.[5]

---

[1] Statute 5 & 6 Will. IV, c. 76, § 66.
[2] MS. Council Minutes, especially 21 Sept. 1836, 19 July 1837.
[3] Ibid. 19 July 1837.
[4] Searson, 60–4.   [5] *ELG*. iii. 481.

IX

THE REPORT OF 1835

NO less tory than the old corporation of Leicester was
the *Annual Register* for 1835. This emphasized that
the report of the municipal commissioners was not unanimous, that one commissioner had dissented entirely, and
another had submitted objections.[1] The objections of Sir
Francis Palgrave were put forward in an 'able and in-
structive document'.[2] By a survey of the evidence offered
in 'the report he was led to the conclusion that, taken as
a whole, the commissioners' findings were in some ways
misleading. The methods of the commissioners had not,
in his view, been such as to produce more than a partisan
report.[3] Particularly, the report failed to distinguish 'ad-
ventitious defects' from 'inherent defects', by which he
meant the sins of individuals from the ingrained weak-
nesses of an obsolete system.[4] It is on this account, in view
of his defence of particular corporations against charges
generally made in the introduction to the report, all the
more significant that he makes no attempt to exculpate
the unreformed corporation of Leicester. Like most of
his contemporaries, he thought chiefly of the 'notorious
case of Leicester in 1826' as having the sole merit of
bringing about the Corporate Funds Act.[5]

Perhaps the most serious charge that can be substantiated
against the old corporation of Leicester is that of financial
mismanagement. 'As administrators of the public funds',
ran the report of 1835, 'it is impossible to speak of the
corporate authorities, except in terms of unqualified cen-
sure. . . . It appears clear that with an income exceeding
4300£ a year, they contribute little or nothing (with the
exception of occasional subscriptions, the amount of which
bears no proportion to their income) to the alleviation of

---

[1] *Annual Register for 1835* (1836), 242.   [2] *ELG.* iii. 721 n.

[3] *House of Commons, Accounts and Papers*, 1835 (4), Protest of Sir Francis
Palgrave, 5.

[4] Ibid.

[5] Ibid. 9. Palgrave here points out that 'no other corporation except Leicester
appears on the face of the printed Report to be charged with this abuse', i.e. using
corporate funds in election purposes.

the heavy local burdens, or to the public institutions or the general improvement of the town, while on the other hand a sum exceeding 1000£ per annum is divided in salaries among the officers of the corporation.'[1] Moreover, the corporation was in debt to the large sum of over £20,000, of which nearly half was the loan from Henry Palmer, and the remainder for the most part incurred by the magistrates on the town jail. The existence of the jail debt, for which a special jail rate was being levied, was not publicly known until the commissioners' inquiry.[2] The finance committee of the reformed corporation could not be sure that the twenty odd thousand pounds was the total debt that it had inherited,[3] and certainly Burbidge made further claims.

Further irregularities appeared in the disposal of some eight thousand pounds raised by the sale of land in the south field. It appeared that, of this, 'three thousand and twenty four pounds ten shillings was received by Mr. R. Rawson and paid under the orders of "the Committee"', while it was also a remarkable fact that there was no reference to the loan of £10,000 from Palmer in any of the corporation bank books, 'and that in none of the corporation books are there any entries of the receipt or appropriation of this large sum'.[4] A good deal of the money not accounted for had plainly been perverted from corporate use by slovenly or unscrupulous members or officers of the corporation. It seems totally impossible to excuse the gross financial laxity revealed by these inquiries. Even if the chamberlains were unpaid and amateur, and perhaps may so far have some excuse,[5] the professional officers of the body had failed in their duty of keeping their employers in the path of financial rectitude. Here more than anywhere else, the old corporate system suffered from the lack of popular control.

---

[1] MCR. 1919.   [2] Ibid.

[3] MS. Council Minutes, 13 Jan. 1836, report of finance committee; £22,770. 15s. 4d. was the total; consisting of £10,000 to Palmer, sums of £10,000, and £225. 13s. 6d. on account of the jail; and £2,545. 1s. 10d. to the firm of Mansfield and Babington.

[4] Ibid. 21 Sept. 1836.

[5] The chamberlains' accounts only record ordinary matters; ibid.

Very largely the financial necessities of the old corporation were the consequence of its determined political
partisanship. Political exclusiveness was made a virtue,
and only on one occasion, so far as can be ascertained,
does the corporation appear to have admitted to the hall
members of 'improper' political opinions.[1] Nobody was
ever admitted to the corporation, according to the report
of 1835, unless of the corporation or tory party, 'however
wealthy, however intelligent, however respectable'.[2] 'No
corporation has ever interfered more extensively or openly
in elections.'[3] Yet, as Palgrave pointed out in 1835 and
Peel had done earlier, the tories were not alone in municipal exclusiveness; so that the rhetoric of the commissioners' report on this vice at Leicester has to be
somewhat discounted.[4]

It was also affirmed by the report that the political zeal
of the corporation had destroyed the judicial impartiality
of the bench of magistrates, who were, moreover, not
distinguished for intelligence or for station.[5] This again
was largely common form in the radical attack on the
unreformed corporations, and Palgrave maintained that
the inquiries made into the working of the town magistra-
cies had been insufficiently precise.[6] It is quite possible
that the complaints made against the Leicester magistrates
were exaggerated, for the commissioners chose to dismiss
evidence offered in defence of the Leicester justices, as
coming from persons of no great opulence,[7] and relegated
mention of an address in their favour to a footnote.[8] None
the less, suspicion was rife in the town, a fact sufficient to
condemn the old system. The report on Leicester quoted
the words of Robert Brewin, 'an enlightened and opulent
inhabitant of Leicester', for the view that 'the system
tends to engender a spirit of insubordination and of resistance to constituted authorities, far more than national

---

[1] *Leicester Journal*, 12 June 1818.   [2] MCR. 1909.
[3] Ibid.
[4] MCR. 1917; the commissioners complained because the parents of boys for
Newton's school voted tory; yet they had to be anglican.
[5] Ibid.; 'not composed of the most eligible persons, either as regards intelligence or station'.
[6] Palgrave, loc. cit. i, 14.   [7] MCR. 1921.   [8] Ibid. 1922 n.

grievances, greater but more distant would do. It is a sore always galling; a disease that visits us by our fireside.'[1]

This picture of the old corporate system has become part of the vulgate of history. So far as Leicester is concerned, even the most judicious of investigators have not challenged it.[2] Certainly it cannot be even largely disproved, but its general impression may be mitigated. For the report is lawyer-like. It is the argument of the prosecuting counsel, who skilfully manipulates the defendant's own words to his utmost discredit.[3] Moreover, the report originated in an atmosphere of heated political contention, intensified by the recent memories of 1826. The commissioners, already wedded to the cause of the reformers, were bound to be carried away in the enthusiasm of battle. It is certain that their antagonism was increased by the corporation's tory devotion to the established church.[4]

The commissioners' report on the Leicester corporation was dominated by the immediate situation; it therefore lacked historical perspective. It was too simple an argument : that because the town was ill-lit and dirty, and the municipality exclusive, blame was due to the existing corporators, and that they could do nothing right. It had not commonly been held the duty of municipal corporations to provide generally for the local government of the towns, after the manner envisaged by the municipal reformers. The recognized duties in the management of corporate property, markets, and charities the corporation of Leicester had performed on the whole in such a way that the value of them all was greatly increased. If in the later part of the period there was little zeal for public improvement in the corporation, it was true also that such efforts as were made received little encouragement. The municipal commissioners themselves had to refer to the factious opposition that ruined the plan of 1822;[5] they

---

[1] MCR. 1921.

[2] *ELG.* iii. 475–81. For a most illuminating view of the general position, see the Webbs' 'alternative judgement', 722–37.

[3] A most damaging feature of the report was its quotation verbatim, supplemented by comments, from documents sent by the corporation.

[4] Cf. the interesting case of Liverpool; *ELG.* iii. 488–9.

[5] MCR. 1921.

failed to give due weight to the difficulties caused by the very small area of the borough magistrates' jurisdiction.

The unreformed corporation of Leicester was in fact very typical of the old system. Its unenviable notoriety partly derived from its usefulness as an illustration of the reformers' thesis. But even so it is of no great value to consider the report on even a very typical municipality without reference to that heterogeneous constitutional structure, of which the corporations formed but a small part. The radical pamphleteer Nicholas Wade had seen that the unreformed corporations were but one of the 'feet of clay on which the tory oligarchy has been borne up'.[1] Thus the abuses that existed in the old corporation of Leicester could be paralleled in more august bodies. The finances of government departments in the eighteenth century were not less designed to the benefit of office-holders than those of the Leicester corporation, while few institutions had a more exclusive spirit, were more jealous of the secrecy of their proceedings, or gave more convincing exhibitions of corporate arrogance than the house of commons itself. Under the pressure of middle-class reformers, the chief supports of the old oligarchy, the unreformed church, the unreformed commons, and the unreformed corporations, all underwent more or less considerable transformation in the first half of the nineteenth century.

The reform of the municipal corporations was, as the case of Leicester particularly clearly shows, the most complete of the triumphs of the middle class. While the house of lords and the rule of the counties, the preserves of the landed gentry, remained substantially unchanged, the fields in which the bankers, merchants, and manufacturers would be most active, the house of commons and the corporations of the great towns, had on the contrary to be adapted to suit their purposes. The 'opulence', the 'intelligence', the 'respectability', to which the municipal commissioners had so often, and so emphatically, referred, were now enfranchised, and in the great towns were dominant. Their triumph brought into practice new ideas of the scope of government, and new standards of public

---

[1] N. Wade, *The Black Book* (1835), 452.

responsibility. The success of this new régime of consumers' control had the result that justice was hardly done to the old corporations. Due allowance was rarely made for the anomalies with which they had had to contend. The benefits which had been conferred by their old-fashioned philanthropy were overlooked. Attention was taken rather by the numerous necessary and admirable public improvements which were undertaken by the reformed municipalities, as well as by the economies which were effected by them, often in a niggardly ratepayer-saving spirit. English town government made a new start, under conditions that seemed to some optimistic Victorians to promise a future of greater freedom and comfort than had been afforded by the unenlightened past.

INDEX